Lesbian Sex Wars

Emma Healey

A *Virago* Book

First published in Great Britain by Virago Press 1996

This collection and introduction copyright © Emma Healey 1996

The moral right of the author has been asserted

A CIP catalogue for this book is available from the British Library

ISBN 1-86049-230-4

Typeset in Sabon by M Rules
Printed and bound in Great Britain by
Clays Ltd, St Ives plc

Virago
A Division of
Little, Brown and Company (UK)
Brettenham House
Lancaster Place
London WC2E 7EN

Emma Healey is a freelance writer. She has worked as a part-time administrator for a lesbian and gay charity and was active in lesbian and gay politics in the 1980s when she regularly wrote for lesbian and gay magazines in both Scotland and the north-west of England. She co-edited *Stonewall 25: The Making of the Lesbian and Gay Community in Britain* (Virago 1994) and has written for the lesbian magazine, *Diva*.

For Jane Held,
with love

Contents

Acknowledgements

Many women, and even a handful of men, made this book possible. Jeni Bremner was a constant source of help and support and helped me to shape many of the ideas in this book. Anya Palmer has twice been my unpaid literary agent and given me much information and encouragement. The support of Jo Bird, Carmel Barr, Yoni Ejo, Amanda Greenwood, Jan Scott, Caroline Healey and Bill Bankes-Jones has been invaluable. Jan Baxandall and Mark Held provided the perfect hideaway where much of this book was written. Ken Batty's sharp eye and clear thinking were always helpful and encouraging. This book simply could not have been written without Jane Held.

Many women gave their time to be interviewed for this book. I would particularly like to thank Lynn Romeo, Jackie Foster, Jean Fraser, Rita O'Brien, Lisa Power, Penny Wallace, Julie Bindel, Cherry Smyth, Maggie Sansom, Evelyn Asante-Mensah, Luchia Fitzgerald, Angela Cooper, Maggie Turner and Francis Williams and the women who agreed to be interviewed but asked to remain anonymous. The Feminist Library in London and the Hall Carpenter Archives at the LSE provided many sources of information for this book; my visits to the Lesbian Archive (now safely stowed in Glasgow) were invaluable. This book would not have been possible without support from the Trustees of the Albert Kennedy Trust, particularly Nick Dearden, Hugh Fell and Kate Williams.

Finally I would like to thank Becky Swift who had the confidence in me to set the ball rolling, and Melanie Silgardo, my editor at Virago, whose patience, forbearance and perceptiveness have been extraordinary.

Introduction

When I was at school we knew all about lesbians. Lesbians taught us sports and lingered in the changing rooms, they led sad and lonely lives with other sad and lonely lesbians. In our all girls' school we might speculate about each other's sexuality, we might even have the odd passionate affair, but we were never lesbians. Even in the 1970s, the word lesbian still conjured up images of misery and depravity.

But in the 1990s, this image has at last begun to change. Lesbianism has become, if not exactly acceptable, then at least a little fashionable. At the beginning of 1995, three out of the four major British soap operas featured strong, positive lesbian characters; Channel Four even gave lesbians *Dyke TV*, their own slot on prime-time TV. Both broadsheet and tabloid newspapers have become fascinated by lesbians and lesbianism. Suddenly, lesbians have found their place in the media sunshine and a heterosexual consciousness.

Yet sometimes I feel as if I am standing on the bridge between two generations of lesbians. The first are the lesbians who, through feminism, gave lesbianism a new validity and a new credibility in a hostile heterosexual world. The second are the new generation of 1990s lesbians who have given lesbianism a chic and a cachet that it has never had before. It would be comforting to see these generations as a part of lesbian evolution, from the shadowy figures lurking in the twilight world of the 1950s and 1960s, to the out, proud, politicised lesbians of the 1970s and early 1980s, to the 1990s lesbians who have abandoned radical politics but have found radical chic. And the last twenty-five years have seen a glorious evolution, and indeed revolution, in how we live our lives as lesbians. Yet too often it seems to me that rather than reconciling ourselves to the various strands of our own history, we make enemies of it. Yesterday's courageous pioneer is tomorrow's *bête noire*, yesterday's political radicalism is tomorrow's political fascism. We are far less excited by the notion of an evolution of lesbian politics, life-styles and ideas than we are by pointing our fingers at which of us is wrong and which of us is right.

The trouble is that though we are happy with the idea that our lesbian and gay sexuality makes us different from our heterosexual brothers and sisters, we are less happy to see that diversity amongst ourselves. We will allow you to be black, white, disabled, Irish, Jewish, working class, etc., but would still prefer it if you would think the same as we do and act the same as we act and dress the same as we dress. Again and again, our movement has been stopped in its tracks by pointless arguments. Just look at the regular rows between the lobbying group Stonewall, and the direct action group, Outrage, and you will see that our most popular slogan no longer seems to be 'Out and Proud' but 'Are you with us or against us?'

But who are we? We are each forged from different backgrounds, histories and experience. Some of us are lesbians from birth, some of us are born again, some of us chose lesbianism, some of us have lesbianism thrust upon us. Whether it be nature or nurture, all we can say is that each experience of our lesbian sexuality will be different from another's. Yet it seems that in the last twenty years or so we have not been content to accept this diversity, rather we have wanted to create a single, acceptable template of how to be a lesbian in a heterosexual world. In the 1970s and early 1980s, as lesbian feminists, we created a political framework that defined lesbianism as a political response to the patriarchal power of heterosexual society. In the 1990s we are less concerned with political complexity and more concerned with creating a lesbian life-style that is both fashionable and sexy. Yet we also seem to want to put a tremendous amount of energy into attacking each generation of lesbian experience. The lesbians of the 1970s and early 1980s were 'too political', 'anti-sex', 'humourless', the lesbians of the 1990s are 'not political enough', 'obsessed with sex', 'naive', while the poor old lesbians of the 1950s and 1960s are either heroines or pariahs.

It is almost as if we do not want to own up to a lesbian history, as this would mean owning up to our mistakes, our little wrong turns and strategic disasters. We forget that our history will also tell us of our little victories, our extraordinary courage and our splendid successes. This century has shown us that we are survivors, that we can adapt and disguise and also stand up, shout loud and fight for what we believe in. But we have to accept that when we turn and criticise those who have gone before us we are not just criticising them but stealing from our own lesbian history. We can not dismiss the butch/femme lesbians of the 1950s and 1960s, nor can we dismiss the lesbian feminists of the 1970s, nor the lesbian bad girls and radical queers of the 1990s. They are all a part of what makes us what we are today.

As feminists and lesbians in the 1970s we created a world of women which, through its anger with and indifference to male power, could challenge and could change. In the early 1980s, lesbians arguably carried the torch for feminism as well as becoming the backbone of the Women's Peace Movement. In the late 1980s lesbians joined with gay men to fight Section 28, but it was lesbians who stormed the citadels, the House of Lords and the BBC. In the 1990s, lesbians have won their space in the spotlight. More lesbians are coming out in their work-places, in their families, on the scene. We have used our differences to good effect. If we were once shut out by our sex-uality, we have now forced our way back in.

But we are still outsiders. No matter that we are on the front covers of fashionable magazines or are the stars of every soap opera worth its name. We know that our fashionable appeal today lies in the fact that we don't quite belong, that we never have quite belonged and that nobody out there really knows what to make of us. And in that situation it makes it very important that we belong to ourselves, that we, at least, know who we are, what we think and how we live. A love affair with the media is like marriage with an abusive hus-band. You never know when the kind words and the polite enquiry will turn to violence, ridicule and pain. That is why, though I can revel in the lesbian sunshine, I miss the political energy of the 1970s and 1980s. We have lost that pro-active energy which made feminism and lesbianism so exciting. We knew that somehow, somewhere, women were changing the world. But oh, what hard work that whole process became. How could we change the wider world when we hadn't quite changed our own yet. Whatever women tell you, there were endless meetings, circular discussions, tiresome arguments; by the mid-1980s we knew all the arguments, all the concerns, we just weren't quite sure about the solutions. In the 1990s, we have lost the pro-active energy for change, we have become re-active. The lesbian activist group, Lesbian Avengers, brings us a sense of humour, glamour and lesbian fun but it will not change the world. The Avengers respond to the homophobia of others, MPs, newspapers, Channel Four, but when they say 'We Recruit', they mean lesbians only. But this is important too, we are adaptable enough to change our strategies and make our presence felt, whatever society throws at us. The lesbian of the 1990s challenges heterosexual assumptions just as effectively as her lesbian feminist foremother did. We may not always like her methods, we may wonder if she is always in control, but to be a lesbian in the 1990s is just as much an act of courage as it was to be a lesbian in the 1900s, the 1950s or the 1970s.

Yet how we have struggled amongst ourselves. In the last twenty-five years we have struggled to find a definition of ourselves that challenges the old ideas of lesbians as sick and bad and sad. Part of that struggle has been to find our own parameters and boundaries so that we can make sense of the lesbian world we live in. But lesbianism does not exist within a vacuum and as the world has changed around us, so we have changed with it. We have found the courage and the opportunity to discuss and explore our sexuality for ourselves. And it is here that we have fought lesbian sex wars. It is here that we have made the bedroom such a battlefield. It is the rows about lesbian sexuality and sexual practice that emerged in the 1980s that I call the lesbian sex wars.

Questions about our sexual practice, what was wrong and what was right, what was allowable, what was forbidden, challenged the heart of the definition of sexuality lesbian feminism had created. Issues like bisexuality, butch/femme role-playing and, most contentiously, sado-masochism began to dominate lesbian discussion. Some women will deny that there were ever lesbian sex wars, they will say that a few angry meetings do not make a battleground and that a few SM dykes do not make an army. But something did change in the 1980s. Love it or hate it, by the end of the decade, a new language of sexuality and a new fashion for sexuality had been created and the voice of one political ideology had been challenged and almost silenced.

This is not a book about SM, but it is a book about lesbian sex. It looks at how lesbians have tried to find an understanding of their lesbian sexuality and their lesbian sexual practice. It shows how these ideas have changed as lesbianism itself has come out of the heterosexist closet. And, love it or hate it, SM remains central to the lesbian sex wars. Lesbian sex wars begin when we begin to question who we are and what we are. In the 1990s we make great play of the fact that we are different, that we are transgressors from society's norms. In the 1970s we knew we were different too, but we had no power. Through feminism and through lesbian activism we began to find that power, and with that power came the confidence to question. And to explore. And it was this exploration that raised the terrible shadow of SM. For, once you discover that you don't need heterosexual society to succeed, you can start questioning its standards and its boundaries and its rules. Suddenly, lesbians discovered there need be no such thing as a lesbian missionary position; lesbian sex had marvellous possibilities.

And if you could make the rules, then you could change the rules and break them too.

Lesbian sex wars are not in themselves big events. They can be made up of books, films, meetings, marches, discussions and demonstrations. But take them altogether and you have a change, a change in perception and a change in ideology. I believe that the arguments about lesbian sex that dominated much of lesbian politics in the 1980s marked a strange coming of age for the lesbian movement. Suddenly we had the space to talk about our sexuality on our own terms, not the terms of a homophobic, patriarchal society. But how well did we really do? When it comes to talking about such a personal issue as lesbian sex, there are really very few wrongs and rights. Sure, we can all agree that sex should be consensual, that it should not degrade, that it should not damage or be violent. But what can you say when a group of women say 'We want to explore the danger, we want to be powerful and we want to be submissive.' For the lesbian feminists of the 1980s, such wishes challenged the heart of their personal beliefs; they wanted to protect women from a path that threatened everything they had constructed lesbianism to be. And they became frightened, and as they became frightened, they became more passionate in their desire to protect the lesbianism they had created, and as they became more passionate they became more angry. But still those women said they wanted to explore that danger. They said it again and they said it louder. They said it in books, in films and at meetings. And as they became more passionate, so they became more angry.

In *Lesbian Sex Wars*, I want to show how two generations of lesbians struggled to gain an understanding of lesbian sex, and how these struggles have informed how we regard lesbian sexuality in the 1990s. I believe that much of the anger that was created within the lesbian community by such controversial issues as SM or butch/femme was fuelled in part by our fear of diversity and difference. In the 1970s and early 1980s we tried to convince ourselves that lesbianism was something so deeply political that you could subsume the personal within it. But whether we like or not, what makes us different from our heterosexual sisters can never be our politics alone; what we do in bed, our lesbian sex, is just as important a part of what makes us what we are. Thus, our discussions of issues like SM are never going to be simply political ones. Arguments about our sexual practice are deeply personal to us. When we disagree about SM it is not just that our political boundaries are reached, it is that our own personal, sexual boundaries are also breached and challenged. In this context, those who are different to us become deeply threatening and any expression of difference is deeply challenging.

But why did the sexual acts of the few impinge upon the politics of the many? For some lesbian feminists, the arrival of new American ideas about lesbian SM in books like *Coming to Power* (Samois 1981), or the 'Sex Issue' of the magazine *Heresies* (1982), were like so many rats bringing the plague of SM to a frightened lesbian world. That lesbians themselves should seek a sexual practice that was violent and male-identified was almost unthinkable. The feminist politics of the time had no space for a sexual practice that played with and replicated patriarchal modes of power. However, it soon became clear that other British lesbians did want to look at lesbian desire a little more closely and they were prepared to explore complicated issues like SM or butch/femme role-playing to do it. But the response of lesbian feminism was deeply defensive: SM was wrong, those who wanted to talk about SM were wrong. The spectre of SM came to lesbianism at a time when women had actually begun to think they had got this lesbian sexuality business sorted. The feminist movements of the 1970s and 1980s had overturned the old sexological definitions of lesbian sexuality. Feminism had created a lesbian sexuality that was loving, supportive and deeply validating. SM with its clear overtones of pain, humiliation and violence seemed too male-identified to countenance. It was this perception of SM as the ultimate in male behaviour that fuelled lesbians' fear of it and opposition to it. And many lesbians did genuinely fear what SM represented for the new lesbian world.

The very defensiveness of those who opposed SM found an answering anger, and indeed defensiveness, in those who either practised SM themselves (and there were lesbians in Britain who did) and those who just believed that the ideas and issues should be discussed more openly. Lesbian feminism had created a platform which said that it was alright to be a lesbian. Suddenly the same group of women were saying it wasn't alright to have certain forms of lesbian sex. As lesbians' confidence in their own sexuality grew, it was inevitable that women would either want to explore or at least discuss, what the boundaries of that sexuality might be. And the boundaries were, of course, deeply personal ones. It is interesting to see how discussions which were supposed to be based on politics became highly personalised. Often debates around SM degenerated into simple name-calling with both sides often using the same names. Thus you could be labelled a fascist for opposing SM or be guilty of fascist behaviour by practising SM. Though the politics of racism, fascism, free speech or libertarianism were frequently summoned up in debate, the very anger and defensiveness of both sides of the argument suggested that this was a deeply personal struggle that had been fought in the hearts and the minds of each individual lesbian present long before the meeting started.

No wonder then, that each side wanted to be right. The sad truth about the lesbian sex wars in the 1980s was that there were no winners and there were no losers. Whilst lesbians had turned their gaze in upon themselves as they argued about sexual politics, the world around them was changing, and changing very rapidly. A decade of Thatcherism was to destroy the collective ethos that fuelled much of the lesbian and indeed feminist activism of the time as new economic pressures and a growing emphasis on individualism took over. But a certain bitterness, and indeed anger, has remained. A sad hangover of the lesbian sex wars has been the re-casting of lesbian feminism not as a political movement of great effectiveness in its time, but as a proscriptive movement that existed to stop lesbians having a good time. At the same time, those who take a more radical sexual stance have themselves been labelled. When the 1990s lesbian is accused of 'having no politics' we should remember that she just has different politics, framed by a different society in a different moment in time.

I do not chose either to deplore lesbian SM or defend it. It is important to point out that throughout the lesbian sex wars and all the rows that centred specifically on SM, it was very difficult to find a single definition of what SM actually is. For some women, SM will always be abusive, a manifestation of male power and men's inherent violence against women, the fact that it is two lesbians practising SM makes no difference. For other women, an understanding that SM is rooted in fantasy and trust makes lesbian SM both possible and fulfill-ing. Thus, SM becomes a manifestation of love and trust, not abuse and violence. For other women still, lesbian SM offers the chance to play at being different, it becomes a powerful statement of a potent lesbian sexuality. What is clear, however, is that we have never been able to reconcile our very different understandings of what lesbian SM is and what it represents.

Nor do I want to condemn the politics of the lesbian femi-nists who were so often opposed to SM. Nor do I believe the arrogance of some sex radical lesbians who want us to believe that only an SM agenda can bring us a true understanding of ourselves. I will be critical of certain commentators, both les-bian feminist and sex radical, I will be critical of some actions and I will be critical of some ideas. But I do believe that les-bianism should, by the end of this millennium at least, have reached the point where it can allow different understandings, different interpretations and different conclusions.

The two most unhelpful phrases conjured up by the lesbian sex wars were 'pro-sex' and 'anti-sex'. The very act of defining yourself as lesbian means you understand that it is your sexual choice that makes you different. But when we label lesbians as anti-sex, we mean they disapprove of SM, as if SM was the only valid expression of a lesbian sexuality. Sex has become incredibly important in the 1980s and 1990s. Gay or straight, it seems you have to be seen to be sexual. Not only must you be having sex, but it must be the best sex ever. Sex has been pack-aged and commodified, it has become street-fashion and a feature in every fashionable magazine. Lesbianism, because it is different, because it is 'other', easily finds a place in the hot-sex lexicon. The danger of all this is that, as lesbians, we put too much emphasis on the importance of what we do in bed.

Lesbianism is much more than sleeping with another woman, it has a historical and a social context. Lesbianism does not exist simply in the bedroom; to be a dyke, out and proud in the workplace, in the family, on the streets is still a deeply radical and political act.

I am very aware that when I talk about the lesbian sex wars, I am talking about the actions and the attitudes of the few, not of the many. Lesbians are not only activists but are spectators too. Many of us have not been involved in arguments or angry meetings, many of us have kept ourselves to ourselves and not changed our sexual dynamics just because some other lesbians tell us to. Many lesbians have not changed their perceptions of SM or butch/femme in the 1990s, nor are they rushing out to buy the latest dildo or the latest sex magazine. Yet that does not mean that we should pretend that the changes we have seen in the perceptions of our sexuality have not happened or do not matter. They do.

For while individual lesbians may not have changed, while lesbians remain as different from each other as they have always been, it is the image of the lesbian that has been so radically altered. The lesbian is no longer bad and sad or drearily political, she is a sassy 1990s fashionable gal. She attracts the media's attention because she is suddenly so sexual. And there's the rub. In a culture that values the sexual, the chic lesbian is tantalisingly different yet really still the same. Her sexuality is merely exotic plumage hiding the nice girl underneath. Lesbian chic is dependent on one image of the lesbian, the one that heterosexual society feels it can control: the feminine. Only when straight society admires the lesbian in all her shapes and sizes – big, small, butch, femme, black, white – will the lesbian have truly found her place in the world. Our new confidence in ourselves and our sexuality, fought for a century and more, suggests that we are already half-way there, but our overwhelming obsession and absorption with our sexual practice is at best a diversion and at worst a political dead end.

In studying the lesbian sex wars, I have tried not to be subjective, but I recognise that looking at sex and sexual politics makes it hard to be objective all the time. I recognise as well that this book is bound to be a little London-centred. Whilst many women throughout Britain may have been aware of and concerned by such contentious issues as SM or butch/femme role-playing, these concerns may not have manifested themselves as lesbian sex wars. In Scotland in the 1980s I remember spending much more time arguing about the twin evils of bisexuality and transexuality than I did on the horrors of SM. Even though I have endeavoured to talk to a wide range of women from a wide range of lesbian communities and have read from a wide range of lesbian sources, I have not reported every meeting or every discussion group, but I have tried to get a flavour of how lesbian sex was, and is, discussed and understood. Women, from all sides of the sexuality spectrum, have been incredibly open about their hopes and fears, their anger and their irritation. Many women have expressed a sadness at what they see as the end of lesbian discussion. As the 1990s have progressed, lesbianism seems much more in the control of commercial forces than a collective lesbian energy. And this privatisation of lesbian sexuality, allowable because it has no real political power, could be limiting.

But I believe that we must accept the changing nature of our lesbian history, even our changing mores. We must not discount our many victories because we dislike how those victories were made. I see no future in the continued revision of our history, the blaming of ideologies and individuals. And as for our sexual practice, I say let's abandon the arguments, the cries from the lesbian feminist wilderness, the 'I'm more excitingly sexual than you.' They just get in the way. If we want to fight battles then let's fight them with the homophobes and the bigots. The lesbian sex wars have changed how we regard ourselves and our sexuality, they form another step in our lesbian evolution. But they were the wrong wars with the wrong targets. Yes, it is important to know what we are and what we can do. But it is wrong to use sex, how we think about it and how we practice it, as the measure of what a good or trendy lesbian should be. I'll be honest with you, I am sick to death of SM, of butch and femme, of lesbians telling me what I should or shouldn't do in bed, so I say 'No more lesbian sex wars', but in the meantime, let battle commence . . .

PART ONE

Marshalling the Forces

Essential Sex

Dangerous definitions and the search for lesbian sexuality

This has been the century of the homosexual. Few people at its beginnings would have imagined that homosexuality would be decriminalised or that lesbians and gay men would become a political force to be reckoned with. There is no doubt that this century has seen a great change both in how homosexuality is perceived and how homosexuals perceive themselves. Lesbianism also has found its place in the spotlight, but ours has been a different struggle, based just as much on our status as women as on our own homosexuality.

Much of the struggle for gay rights in the last thirty years has been based around the notion of decriminalising gay sex and equalling the age of consent with that of heterosexuals. The Labouchère Amendment of 1885, which first criminalised homosexual acts between men, made no mention of lesbian sex. However, lesbians have shared, and do share, in the homosexual oppression that legal inequality and injustice have created. It is, then, rather surprising that in 1994 a group of lesbians seriously discussed the idea of campaigning for a specifically lesbian age of consent. In the words of an old feminist Christmas card, 'You don't have to be a turkey to know you're oppressed', but these lesbians saw that there could actually be advantages in placing lesbianism on the statute books.

What this group of lesbians was looking for was the cure for a particularly lesbian disease, lesbian invisibility. They argued that lesbianism's lack of legal (or illegal) status rendered lesbianism invisible in law. This invisibility left lesbians without status and excluded them from the heterosexual consciousness. This not only allowed lesbianism to be ignored and discounted but also robbed lesbianism of coherent political goals.

It is the demand for equality between gay men and heterosexuals, sometimes shouted, sometimes whispered, that has brought gay rights into the national consciousness. The unequal age of consent for gay men is the most potent, damaging and murderous weapon in heterosexual society's arsenal, because it damns gay men for the thing that makes them different. And what makes them different is not their sense of dress, nor their taste in music, but who they have sex with. But ironically, gay men's sexuality is actually recognised and its validity stressed by the legal oppression that it brings. In the light of this, the lesbian search for an age of consent looks to be less about visibility and more about validation.

What makes lesbians different from our heterosexual sisters, whether we like it or not, is the fact that we have sex with women. But because our sexuality has never been recognised in law, lesbianism and lesbian sex become very easy to sweep under the patriarchial carpet. Not only is lesbian sex ignored but it is also trivialised by this omission. A lesbian age of consent would not only redress the balance but would provide a clear recognition, and indeed definition, of lesbian sex and sexuality. With this definition, it was argued, would come recognition of lesbianism as a valid sexuality.

Throughout this century, there have been a number of attempts to define a lesbian sexuality. I would argue that it is the need to define, and the struggle to redefine, our own sexuality that has lain at the heart of the lesbian sex wars. For sexuality gives us a sense of both who we are and where we are in our world, as well as providing us with parameters and rules. I would agree with those who point out the over-importance our century has placed on sexuality, how it has been used both to control and suppress, despite its many inconsistencies. As lesbians – women who choose to break the sexuality rules – we know how sexuality has been used against us, leaving us outside society and silencing our voice. At the same time, those who have chosen to define lesbianism as a purely political stance allow lesbianism to become desexualised and deprive it of some of its power. It is important to remember that the lesbian is as equally threatening a sexual animal as she is a political one.

To understand the lesbian sex wars, we must look at how one group of lesbians began to redefine their sexuality on totally new terms, how they overturned what they considered essentially male definitions of lesbianism as sickness and as taint. I shall call this group of women the lesbian feminists. In fact, during the 1970s and 1980s, lesbian and feminist politics were described as revolutionary or radical feminism, or political lesbianism, but fundamental to all of them was the belief that it was male power that oppressed women and that lesbianism offered a potent political weapon in its overthrow. As the 1980s progressed a newer and more sexually radical generation of lesbians challenged the old lesbian feminist idea as they sought a new lesbian sexual freedom. This formed the battlefield of the lesbian sex wars. Questions about what is and is not lesbian sex became strangely muddled with questions about who is and is not a lesbian. The bizarre result of all this sex war was, that by 1994, lesbians no longer sought to make their own definition of lesbian sexuality and sex, but actually wanted heterosexual society to do it for them.

It was the new science of sexology that was to give lesbianism its first defining identity. In 1864, Karl Ulrichs published a pamphlet which posited the existence of a third sex – that of a male soul trapped in a female body for lesbians and a female soul in a male body for homosexual men. For Ulrichs, this 'inversion' was innate and therefore should not be regarded as sin but more like an accident of hereditary. It was the sexologists Richard von Krafft-Ebing and Henry Havelock Ellis who, following Ulrichs' work, created the defining lesbian identity – the sick, sad lesbian. Both men cast love between women in a highly morbid light and further developed the notion of the lesbian invert, her homosexuality being some sort of congenital defect or 'taint'. Trotting out case-studies of the doomed 'invert' poised either to murder her lover or poison herself, Havelock Ellis and his ilk enjoyed a veritable orgy of speculation and conjecture under the guise of scientific study. If they did not create the lesbian, they certainly shaped a lesbian identity remarkably effectively. The cross-dressing, cigar-smoking, degenerate pseudo-man was born.

Sigmund Freud introduced a new, psychoanalytic theory of homosexuality. He did not agree with notions of degeneracy or taint but placed the emphasis of the creation of the homosexual on nature and nurture. He created the concept of lesbianism as being the result of some sort of 'arrested development' in the child, later suggesting the link between lesbianism and 'penis envy'. However, though Freud did not himself believe homosexuality could be cured, he opened the door to those scientists who did. The cumulative effect of the science of sexology, though this was not always the intention of the individual sexologists involved, was to reinforce the notion of the sick, sad homosexual. The lesbian, in her position as woman and outsider, was to fare particularly badly in this construct.

Lesbian feminist academics have been particularly and understandably scathing about the misogyny of much sexology. The lesbian historian and writer Lillian Faderman sees the sexologist's work as an attack against the growing feminism of the times.

> . . . Those opposed to women's growing independence now could hurl, with credible support behind them, accusations of degeneracy at females who sought equality, and thereby scare them back to the hearth with fears of abnormality.[1]

This suggests that somehow the sexologists created lesbianism as a way of getting their own back on independent women. There were lesbians there before the sexologists, and as Jeffrey Weeks in his book *Sexuality and its Discontents* suggests, the sexologists were in fact trying to 'explain such manifestations, not create them'.[2] Indeed, though it is important not to judge the sexologists on our own terms, we must not underestimate the effects that their theorising had on lesbians and lesbianism, both in their own times and in ours. It is also clear that Havelock Ellis, who in fact advocated a certain toleration towards male homosexuality, was more bothered by the concept of lesbianism. For him, lesbians remained trapped in their 'man in a woman's body' inversion, those who didn't live up to that stereotype, he suggested, had been converted by an active invert. It is interesting to see how these ideas, often based less on information and more on speculation, remain ingrained in the bigot's consciousness.

Some lesbians actually embraced the notion of the lesbian invert. Women have always tried to make the best of the scant resources men have lumbered them with, and here at last was an 'off the peg' definition of their difference that many lesbians could identify with. The whole notion of the sick lesbian, victim of internal or external forces outside her control, could be both a cry for sympathy and a warning to leave well alone. No longer having to force themselves to conform to society's rules, some lesbians found an excuse to be the outsider and thus discovered a path to their own survival.

It is not surprising then that Radclyffe Hall's *The Well of Loneliness*[3] should rely rather heavily on the sexology's interpretation of the lesbian invert. *The Well* is the lesbian book of the century and its heroine, Stephen Gordon, the quintessential lesbian invert. Attempts to stop its publication in 1928 guaranteed its notoriety and therefore its success. In Stephen Gordon it was Hall's clear intention to create a heroine who was to be pitied but not abhorred. Stephen is a victim of her own inversion, a man trapped in a woman's body condemned to strive for a happiness that she can never attain. And so on, and so on. Never has the misery of lesbian existence been so marvellously recreated, never has prose been more leaden. While most lesbians have at one point or another obtained a copy of *The Well of Loneliness*, few of us can bear to read it;

it is a phase all lesbians have to go through, like coming out to parents, or buying your first k.d. lang album.

And because it is such a major piece of lesbian iconography, while at the same time reinforcing such a negative view of our sexuality, *The Well of Loneliness* will always be distinctly problematic. It remains one of the only lesbian classics and dyke after dyke will quote her first formative lesbian experience as being its buying, reading or discarding. And yet most of us will also say we hate it. Such is its power as an emblem of ourselves that we fail totally to be objective in our judgement of it. Our need to be validated by what we read is too strong and our expectations much too high. It is not Radclyffe Hall's fault that reading *The Well* is the equivalent of watching *Basic Instinct* – it represents neither who we are nor what we are.

At the time of *The Well*'s publication, many lesbians were at best ambivalent and at worst actively hostile to it. Some were appalled by its negativity, others were relieved to see themselves depicted in genuine literature at last, still others just wanted to keep their heads down. There is no doubt that the publication of the book did help fuel a lesbian 'scare' – the polite world of the 'romantic friendship' that the researches of Lillian Faderman revealed would never be the same again.[4] The book, for all its faults, certainly took the lid off lesbian sexuality, and the subsequent obscenity trial gained the book widespread publicity and notoriety. Virginia Woolf, who had herself had a lesbian affair with Vita Sackville-West, decried it for its 'meritorious' dullness, but at the same time was one of the defence witnesses at the trial (though the defence witnesses were never allowed to give their evidence). The result of the trial was that *The Well of Loneliness* was found to be obscene, although after various appeals this decision was eventually overturned. However, the book, whilst enjoying great success abroad, was not published again in Britain until 1949.

In Stephen Gordon, Radclyffe Hall's troubled heroine, we also have the prototype butch. All slicked-back hair and natty suiting, Stephen is the sexologists' wet dream. What could be badder, sadder and more dangerous to know than the cross-dressing invert trying to be a man? Freud dearly loved a good butch too, of course. He was so desperate to hang on to the notion of the lesbian as pseudo-man that he concluded that even when a lesbian did not actually look butch, she was probably having butch thoughts: 'Some of her intellectual attributes could be connected with masculinity . . . her acuteness of comprehension and her lucid objectivity.'[5] It is clear that it is the breaking of the male perogative of masculinity that Freud found of most concern. Stephen Gordon is both the inheritor of early sexology and one of its leading examples.

There is no easy moment in history when an 'invert' became a 'butch', but it is the linking of the butch both to manliness and manly behaviour and to the medicalised and pathologised invert, that makes the butch such a contentious figure in our lesbian history.

Some lesbian academics have come close to blaming sexology for the creation of the lesbian, even though, for example, the British diarist Anne Lister, writing in the eighteenth century, created a vivid picture of her active, and specifically lesbian, sexuality long before the likes of Krafft-Ebing, Havelock Ellis and Freud came upon the scene. However, I believe that these academics are quite right to point out the misogyny lying behind much of the sexologists' theorising. Lesbians were threatening to men (and remain so) because they stepped directly into that great shrine of masculinity – the bedroom. The sexologists had neither the imagination nor the inclination to believe that women could be so in control of their sexuality as to choose to have sex with other women. Such an extraordinary idea was so far outside their understanding that, as men of science, they had to find scientific and therefore medical, explanations.

None of this helps the butch lesbian of course. Lesbian feminists have generally been either actively hostile or silently ambivalent about the butch, while other dykes have been more sympathetic to their struggles and found them, I suspect, rather sexy. From the 1920s up to the early 1970s, the butch drove society's perception of what a lesbian is. Feminist lesbians are uncomfortable with the notion that there are women who can play at being men. They are not particularly sympathetic to the idea that butch was, and is, a necessary survival instinct or that butch can have a role in identification and recognition. Just like the sexologists, they see butches as simply pseudo-men. They are equally uncomfortable with the concept of the femme. Who are worse, the women who try to ape male power or the women who play with notions of the worst sort of female weakness? Most importantly, they see butch as perpetuating the old sexologists' myths. Indeed, the fact that butch has remained such an effective dress code for so much of the twentieth century suggests that they might have a point. While we, poor lesbians, lived through the twilight world of the homosexual (*circa* 1928–70), dressed in our natty suits or frilly dresses, society was, at best, actively ignoring us or, at worst, portraying us as certainly unnatural and sometimes positively vampiric.

If in the early part of this century we lesbians were sick and sad, by the middle of it we had become positively evil. In the

1920s and 1930s, whilst literary lesbians such as Natalie Barney, Djuna Barnes and Gertrude Stein were busy swanning around giving lesbianism the sort of chic that quite puts Beth Jordache in the shade, popular literature was casting lesbianism in a much more dangerous light. By the 1950s, in certain shocker novels, no girl was safe from the rapacious lesbian, a creature who would bring defilement to the most innocent flower before dying horribly, and quite deservedly, for her sins.

In reality, there was at this time (if you could find it), an active underground lesbian and gay scene, even though elsewhere lesbianism and lesbians remained largely in the shadows. A number of American novels of the 1960s try to present lesbians and lesbian life in a more positive light. In the mid-1960s Maureen Duffy wrote *The Microcosm*,[6] a vivid re-creation of the underground world of the lesbian bar scene and a plea for lesbians to leave the ghetto. Her characters are intelligent and sensitive and the book manages to be both evocative and hopeful. Ann Bannon, writing in America in the early 1950s, created a lesbian world that was no less evocative, while the Beebo Brinker series of novels depict another underground world, but one with even more dusty bars and broken hearts. There is not much chance of acceptance, let alone happiness and understanding, here:

> I know most of the girls in here. I've probably slept with half of them. I've lived with half of the half I've slept with. I've loved half of the half I've lived with. What does it all come to? . . . You know something, baby? It doesn't matter. Nothing matters. You don't like me, and that doesn't matter. Some day maybe you'll love me, and that won't matter either. Because it won't last. Not down here,

not anywhere in the world if you're gay. You'll never find
peace, you'll never find love.[7]

In Britain, the 1960s saw the creation of the first lesbian social
organisations and the launch of magazines *Arena* and, its successor, *Sappho*. Sappho also arranged social evenings, as did
Kenric (originally the Kensington and Richmond Group), who
launched the first real lesbian network. Through magazines
and meetings both political and social dialogue became possible. Through this, by the early 1970s lesbians were beginning to
reassess their attitudes towards role-playing – although sex
remained somewhat under the covers: 'Oh, we never talked
about *it*', the founder of Kenric was once heard to utter.

The formation of networks, like Kenric and Sappho and
others like them, were important. The medicalisation of lesbianism had led to its isolation from mainstream society and
lesbians themselves were often isolated from each other. It was
only when women started meeting together as lesbians that
they could begin to think about how society treated them and
regard their place in that society. At the same time, research by
pioneers like Alfred Kinsey had begun to question some of the
myths around homosexuality. The Kinsey Reports of 1948 and
1953 were not only revealing about female sexuality by com-
parison with men, but also suggested that up to 28 per cent of
women had erotic responses to other women. This rather put
in question the idea that lesbians were a degenerate species
who existed as freaks on the fringes of society. Kinsey began
the long process of changing society's understanding of the
psychiatry of homosexuality, though it is rather depressing to
note that in 1996 there are still a number of prominent psychi-
atrists who believe that homosexuality is a sickness.

In 1970, the birth of the Gay Liberation Front changed the face of homosexuality. Suddenly lesbians and gay men adopted a political stance that neither accepted shame nor asked politely for pity. Gays and lesbians replaced this negativity with the notion that 'Gay is Good'. At the same time, a new perception was growing among lesbians about their own potential power. In Britain they quickly established a new voice all of their own:

> We share the experiences of our gay brothers but as women we have endured them differently. Whereas the men in GLF partake of the privileges of the male – you have been allowed to learn to organise, talk and dominate – we have been taught not to believe in ourselves, in our judgement, but to act dumb and wait for a man to make the decisions. As lesbians, 'women without men', we have always been the lowest of the low. Only through acting collectively can we overcome our own passivity and your male chauvinism so that together we – the whole GLF can smash the sexist society which perverts and imprisons us all.[8]

Though GLF may not have lasted much longer than these noble sentiments, another important political movement was growing that would have vast significance for lesbians and lesbianism. The birth of the Women's Liberation Movement (WLM) and the rise of feminism irreversibly changed women's notions of themselves and their relationships with men and with male society. As women began to question the role of patriarchy in their lives so they began to make for themselves the space to discuss and explore the issues that previously had remained closed to them. Sex and sexual relationships were clearly going to be on the agenda. The Women's Liberation Movement gave lesbians their first real space to talk about themselves and their sexual feelings. As in previous movements towards feminism, some men did try to raise the spectre of hairy-legged lesbianism as a way of scaring women away, but the WLM established women's right to determine their own sexuality, and the end of discrimination against lesbians became one of the seven demands of the WLM.

Throughout the history of the WLM in Britain, there was much discussion of the role of lesbians and lesbianism within feminism. By the end of the 1970s, however, a new movement had begun to grow within feminism called lesbian feminism, combining with it the notion of political lesbianism. The political theory of lesbian feminism transformed lesbianism from a stigmatised sexual practice into an idea and a political practice that posed a challenge to male supremacy and its basic institution of heterosexuality:

> . . . we were constructing a new feminist universe. Starting with consciousness-raising, in an atmosphere of great optimism, we re-labelled lesbianism as a healthy choice for women based upon self-love, the love of other women and the rejection of male oppression. Any woman could be a lesbian.[9]

By the 1990s many lesbians rejected the highly laudable ideals that lesbian feminism espoused. What could be wrong with defining lesbianism as a healthy choice, rejecting patriarchal oppression? When Adrienne Rich wrote *Compulsory Heterosexuality* in 1982, she coined the phrase 'lesbian

continuum'. For her, lesbianism was not primarily about physical love between women but was a reflection of women's
linking together to overcome a definition of themselves that
was based on their sexual and emotional relationships with
men:

> I mean the term lesbian continuum to include a range . . .
> of women-identified experience; not simply the fact that a
> woman has had . . . genital sexual experience with another
> woman. If we expand it to embrace many more forms of
> primary intensity between and among women . . . we
> begin to grasp breadths of female history and psychology
> which have lain out of reach as a consequence of limited,
> almost clinical, definitions of lesbianism.[10]

Lesbian feminism thus created a definition of lesbianism
which was nothing whatsoever to do with lesbians or lesbian
sex. It was rather like marketing engine oil as washing powder.
The lesbian feminists did overturn the old male definitions of
lesbianism created by the sexologists, but they replaced them
with a notion of lesbianism that seemed to be both idealised
and desexualised.

> We do think that all feminists can and should be political
> lesbians. Our definition of a political lesbian is a woman-
> identified woman who does not fuck men. It does not
> mean compulsory sexual activity with women.[11]

Pity . . . Mind you, lesbian feminism had to avoid creating a
sexual identity for lesbians since all definitions on sexual
grounds alone must, *ipso facto*, be male-defined and therefore

patriarchal. Oh, for Sheila Jeffrey's certainty when it comes to explaining what or who a lesbian is:

> Lesbian feminists do not tend to seek an explanation because they do not see lesbianism as a minority condition but as a positive choice for all women.[12]

But this is primarily a politically, not sexually, positive choice for women. The great criticism of the lesbian feminist approach is that by making lesbianism a political tool in the overthrow of male power, lesbianism remains strangely male-identified. It is a strategy against male power rather than a positive choice for women.

Lesbian feminism takes it for granted that lesbianism must be socially constructed. However, the 1980s and 1990s some lesbians began to question this certainty and the continuing fascination with butch/femme lesbianism led some women to wonder whether lesbianism could be innate. The idea that lesbians might be born butch or born femme is a deeply contentious one that we are really no closer to resolving than we were twenty years ago, or indeed a century ago. Whether we think that lesbianism is a result of nature or nurture, it has become much easier to attack lesbian feminists for the truly great sin of the late twentieth century – not being nearly sexual enough. Indeed, some lesbians have gone on to criticise lesbian feminists for being anti-sex or some sort of lesbian sex-police. Lesbian feminists did not seek a rigid lesbian sexual identity but some women have felt that they created a rigid code of sexual behaviour:

> Looking back on my first experiences of coming out . . . it

soon became clear that sex wasn't a statement of desire, it was a political belief. I knew the personal was political, but I needed the physical to affirm my new identity. I can't have been the only dyke in town whose cunt came out before her consciousness.

. . . I thought that by coming out I would regain control and reclaim my sexual desires, but sex, which I had always thought was a personal and private experience, had become a prescribed activity, choreographed by the radical lesbian collective.[13]

Is this paranoia? If it is, many of the women I spoke to seem to share it, whilst others seem totally bewildered by it. Everard's comments tell us much more about the group of lesbians she was interacting with at the time than they do about lesbian feminist ideology. There is often a great difference between lesbians' experience of lesbian feminism and the ideology itself. In later chapters we will look at some of the myths and some of the realities of how lesbians have regarded each other, and each other's politics, during the lesbian sex wars.

In the 1980s and 1990s the lesbian movement has become dominated by conflict around issues of sexual practice like SM and butch/femme role-playing. It is here that we have most vigorously fought the lesbian sex wars. We will be looking at these skirmishes in later chapters. However, it is clear that there has been a shift in lesbian attitudes to issues like SM over the last ten years. By the early 1980s the WLM had fallen apart and lesbian feminism had largely taken over as the dominating, feminist and lesbian ideology. At the same time, SM began to be a point of discussion for many lesbians interested in exploring their sexuality further. It was largely the lesbian feminists who led the opposition to what they saw as a rise in SM within the lesbian and gay scene. By the late 1980s lesbian feminism itself had become discredited and the pro-sex, pro-SM brigade seemed to have gained political ascendancy. In the early 1980s lesbian feminists would say that SM oppressed lesbians, women of colour, women who experienced violence. By the late 1980s to early 1990s the pro-sex lobby would accuse the lesbian feminists of themselves being the oppressors.

This shift in emphasis is important since it marks a major change in how lesbians regard their sexuality. Newer lesbians, coming out in the 1990s, are as far away from the politics of feminism as New Labour is from socialism. They see themselves as feminists but their feminism grows from individualism rather than the collectivism that their older sisters once espoused.

However, if the 1990s lesbian is denying the lesbian feminist political identity, she is less certain what particular identity she is replacing it with. Is it really good enough to base a whole sexuality on what you do in bed – not necessarily even who you do it with, but whether you wear leather, flourish a dildo or whether you call yourself a top or a bottom? Lesbianism in the 1990s does seem to be much more about life-style and sex-style than it does about political belief.

The notion that lesbianism is nothing more than a life-style choice and therefore something that could be highly commodified, has been growing since the mid-1980s. Indeed, some lesbian writers have been quick to see the weakness of such ideas.

For many women whose first understanding of their own

lesbianism took place in the context of the pathological
model, the 'life-style' alternative has offered an important
means of self-identification, and the label 'homophobia'
has offered both an explanation of and a weapon against
hostility towards lesbianism . . . the 'life-style'
interpretation of lesbianism individualises and
depoliticises the lesbian threat, just as effectively as did
the . . . 'pathological' model.[14]

Lesbian feminism is based on the notion that our sexuality
is controlled and constructed by outside forces – the forces of
male patriarchy. The French philosopher Michel Foucault
also believed in the social construction of the homosexual
and, indeed, has been described as the father of social construction. He believed that it is power that drives the
workings of society. In the nineteenth century power became
symbolised and controlled by regulation, therefore concepts
like good and evil become less about what is right or wrong
and more about what is normal and abnormal. When the
sexologists established notions of abnormality and normality
around sexual behaviour, they therefore created the homosexual.

Foucault's ideas have been used to show how notions of the
rights and wrongs of individual sexual behaviour can be used
to police, and indeed oppress, groups within a society.
Whereas lesbian feminists believe that male power is at the
core of women's oppression and that, therefore, manifestations of male sexual power (including SM and sex role-playing)
are themselves abusive and oppressive, an analysis based on
Foucault can actually suggest that the forbidding of certain
sexual practices is nothing more than a way for society to

restrict and regulate our behaviour. Lesbian feminists therefore become the oppressors, forcing their beliefs of good and evil, wrong and right, on a lesbian nation – desperate, no doubt, to get out their dildos. For those sex radicals, Foucault provides access into new ideas about demolishing old notions of sexuality and creating new ones.

This fits in very nicely with the new queer sexuality and polymorphous perversity of the 1990s. Queer has been welcomed by some and greeted with confusion by others. Queer puts the sex into sexuality and demands an up-front language of lesbian sex. It also allows lesbians to play around with sexuality on their terms.

> Now some of us are more confident and able to play with notions of gender. We are not afraid that if we use a dildo we are aping heterosexual sex. We have permission to exchange power.[15]

Shock horror, some lesbians even have sex with gay men. Now some cynics say that this is just having your cake and eating it (something bisexuals have never been allowed to get away with). Nevertheless, queer allows lesbians to explore their sexuality in a way that lesbian feminism never could. Queer also relies on a definition of sexuality that is highly sexual. Its politics is its use of the sexual to illustrate power dynamics and to challenge both hetero- and homosexual mores. But who is really interested? The lesbian and gay movement is always good at sending itself internal memos – what could be more internal than a politics based on sex? Lesbian feminism, for all its worthiness, its touchy-feely politics, at least aims at higher targets.

Our new lesbian sexuality may be about doing what you want to who you want, being out and out and proud as a 1990s dyke, but to take us back to the lesbian age of consent debate, some of us may feel that isn't quite enough. I do believe that in this century lesbians have radically altered their understanding of their own sexuality. But in our search to define just what our lesbian sexuality is, some of us have tried to fence in and limit our sexuality through rules and regulations, do's and don'ts. It is here we have rebelled and here where we have come to blows. For the other side of our search for a sexuality is our failure to sort out what sex really means for our lives. When sexuality is our field of battle, it is sex that provides the weapons. Thus, issues like whether we role-play in the bedroom or have SM fantasies we play out in our sexual lives, take on a quite disproportionate importance.

SM, butch and femme role-playing, and bisexuality are all issues that have brought conflict to lesbian politics. They threaten our notions of what lesbianism and lesbian sex can, and should, be about. In the early 1980s we couched our fear of these threats in strictly political terms. SM was linked to violence and fascism, butch and femme aped the worst forms of heterosexist behaviour, bisexuality was the worst form of fence-sitting. Many women I have spoken to argue that the use of politics to police the bedroom is fundamentally dishonest. They believe that much of the fear around these 'dangerous' behaviours is based on our failure to understand and communicate what sex really means in our lives.

Lesbians are not alone in this sexual silence. There has been much discussion among heterosexual feminists about finding an understanding of sex and indeed, love.

Some lesbian sex radicals have recently urged straight women 'to come out of the closet'. We're still waiting, they complain, for you to discuss your sexuality . . . As usual silence greeted their challenge. It is a silence I have come to expect. For feminists with longer memories, however, and those who have lustily resisted the sound of and fury of the last fifteen years, it is a strange phenomenon. How, they might ask, did a movement which came out of and drew its initial strength from the assertive sex radicalism and utopian thinking of the 1960s counter-culture manage to produce so many who would end up so silent on questions of sex and love.[16]

Many would argue that women have been effectively socialised into a state of being unable to talk about their sexual needs and demands. Heterosexual sex has been seen to demand both the passivity of women and their acquiesence to whatever sexual demands men may make upon them. Women, thus, have denied both the power and the language to speak their desires.

But it becomes rather more confusing when lesbians say that they do not have the language to express their sexual fears and their sexual fantasies either. Lesbians and lesbianism do not exist in a vacuum – we have been equally as socialised as our heterosexual sisters. But surely the lesbian feminist movement gave lesbians the perfect opportunity and environment to sort all this sex business out? However, a definition of lesbianism as merely a response to the power of patriarchy, a lesbian as someone 'who does not fuck men' does leave a dialogue about lesbian sex out in the cold.

And what is lesbian sex? Is it something emotional that

you do with your politically sussed sister or is it some highly elaborate scene involving a stranger, a dildo and a passing gay boy? This lack of definition becomes particularly important for lesbians when they began to argue about issues of sexual practice. What for example, is SM? Is it about unleashing our hidden desires and fantasies in the safest possible arena, or is it a dangerous collusion with the heterosexual world that threatens the very temple of idealised sexuality? And what makes SM? Is it sex toys, whips and chains, or is it penetrating your partner with one finger, two fingers, maybe your whole fist? Some women I have spoken to have waggishly described SM 'as anything that you yourself feel uncomfortable with'. Whatever our own definition, a political definition of sex that denies the sexual person within us does make it all too easy to describe any sexual practice we personally find threatening or difficult as heterosexist and politically 'dangerous'.

It is quite understandable that we lesbians have wanted a definition of our own sexuality. It is important to be able to make sense of our own world and it is important to have some rules by which we can live. Elizabeth Wilson in her essay 'I'll Climb The Stairway to Heaven' writes, 'Sexual identity and sexual desire are not fixed and unchanging. We create boundaries and identities for ourselves to contain what might otherwise threaten to engulf, or dissolve into formlessness'.[17] I believe this is highly relevant when we discuss emotive issues like SM or butch and femme role-playing. For while we have, at times, been keen to show how these issues affect us on a political level, we have been less keen to show how they threaten and even excite us on a more personal level.

Sex can be a dangerous business. As individuals we all have

our own sexual boundaries. The stretching of these boundaries can be as frightening as it can be exciting. Yet it is very
difficult to find a safe space to give these fears or difficulties
an airing outside of a bedroom. We can only look to our partners to tell us whether or not what we do or don't do is
'alright'. This affirmation is not always enough. Some of the
1990s sex radicals might claim that they have created an up-
front atmosphere that both allows discussion of previous
sexual taboos and opens the bedroom door of lesbian sex. I
am not so sure. I believe a lot of the posturing around sexuality is simply posturing. It is as hard today to talk about what
we can do and what we won't do as in the 1980s. Lesbian sex
today may have a highly public persona, but it is as private as
it has ever been.

If in the late 1970s and early 1980s our definition of who we
are was based on who we didn't fuck, then in the 1990s our
definition seems to be based squarely on the notion that all we
do is fuck. In the 1990s, it seems to be incredibly important to
say you have sex. But it is not enough to say you are sexual, you
can't just have sex, you have to have great sex. The media's
recent flirtation with lesbian chic is precisely because it has
picked up on lesbian fashion for up-front sexuality. But on
just whose terms? The media loves the image of the fashion-
conscious, chic lesbian, just because she is so unthreatening.
She brings no nasty political posturing, she just wants to party.
She may be 'in yer face' but all she's going to do is wiggle her
bottom.

But the pressure for lesbians to be sexual, and to be seen to
be sexual, can be as limiting as the pressure to be political and
be seen to be political. In this case, at least modern 'sextastic'
lesbians have a strange amount in common with their feminist

lesbian foremothers. For one group the pleasure is political, for the other the political is the pleasure. In both world views, our needs and wants, our questions and our fears, may well be skated over and forgotten while other imperatives find the spotlight.

Before We Knew Any Better

Butch and femme

What does a lesbian look like? These days she could be the winsome character in a weekly soap opera or the pouting model in *Vogue* magazine. She could be the fashion-conscious babe in a London nightclub or the tired old feminist still going to political meetings. There are myriad different lesbian identities, but one has continued to trouble and inspire us. She has a contentious place in our history and in our consciousness. She is the butch.

Lesbian fashions may come and go, but you can bet your bottom dollar that the butch will always be there.

Butch babes . . . are also very practical. If you invite one into your house, she will have the back off your tumble dryer in seconds. Night-table reading matter includes motorcycle manuals. Her partner may be a 'femme'. At nightclubs, butch babes tend to buy the drinks, and always stand with one foot propped up on the bar stool, one arm round their girlfriend, the other hand deep in jean pocket, fiddling with a Swiss army pocket-knife.[1]

So this is the mannish lesbian, 1990s style. This *Sunday Times*' 'butch babe' carries the weight of nearly one hundred years of stereotyping on her shoulders. Even in the lesbian chic 1990s, it is clear that the butch still has the power to frighten hetero-sexist newspapers into scorn and ridicule. But who are the butches and the femmes and why can the Big Ugly Dyke still pack a powerful lesbian punch? And why did butch and femme role-playing become one of the battlegrounds of the lesbian sex wars?

In the previous chapter we saw how the sexologists of the late nineteenth and early twentieth century pathologised lesbianism, turning it into sickness and a 'taint'. They created the notion of the 'invert' – the woman so trapped in a man's body that she would dress like a man, think like a man and even have sex like a man (i.e. with women). Radclyffe Hall's *The Well of Loneliness* seemed to buy the sexologist's line. For her, the embracing of a definition of sexuality that medicalised lesbianism, and in effect turned it into a third sex, the invert, could be used as a method of gaining, if not society's support for the lesbian, then at least its sympathy.

Sigmund Freud brought a whole new side to the debate about lesbian sexuality: it was still clearly to be seen as a sickness, but it was not a congenital one – it was nurture, not nature. He thus dispensed with the notion of the congenital invert, though interestingly he did not see that homosexuality could ever be cured. Like Radclyffe Hall, however, he did see two distinct roles for the lesbian: the pseudo-male (or invert), and her feminine partner – the prototype butch and femme.

It is interesting, but not surprising, to note that the sexologists were much more taken with a study of the butch than they were with the femme. The femme could easily be explained away: there was something missing in her make up, she was either too ugly or too innocent to find a proper man. Or she was just visiting and would return to the arms of happy heterosexuality when rescued by a proper man. The sexologist's perception of the powerlessness of femininity rendered the femme unthreatening and uninteresting, whereas the butch, with her masculine ways and her masculine clothes, proved infinitely more problematic.

It is deeply ironic that what rendered the butch lesbian threatening to the sexologists in the early part of this century rendered her equally as threatening to the lesbian feminists in the 1980s. Nothing could be more threatening than the notion of women adopting and enjoying male roles and privileges. We have seen how accusations of lesbianism could be used to stymie women's efforts towards gaining freedom and influence. The sexologists did not pathologise lesbians and lesbianism solely to stop a feminist revolution, but the unfortunate side-effect of their medicalisation was to render lesbianism so dangerously 'other' that it could be used as a weapon. More importantly, perhaps, the image of the lesbian as sick, sad, bad and dangerous to know has stayed with us for most of the century, to the point, it seems, that some lesbians even believe it themselves. There has been a tendency in some feminist circles not to understand the butch and the femme in the context of their own time and society, but to blame and attack them from within a different context. Whilst butch and femme lesbians of previous decades were living in an oppressive society and through their adherence to male/female roles, sometimes reflected that oppression in their groupings, they were also leading specifically lesbian lives – the feminism could come later.

But what did the butch lesbian in the early part of the century actually look like? There she is with her fine cheek-bones, her gentlemen's suits and that slicked-back hair, smoking that fine cigar, or better still, as in Richard von Krafft-Ebings' description of Mrs von T . . .

> Her love of sport, smoking and drinking, her preference for clothes cut in the fashion of men, her lack of skill in and liking for female occupations, her love of study or obtuse and philosophical subjects, her gait and carriage, severe features, deep voice, robust skeleton, powerful muscles and absence of adipose layers have the stamp of masculine character.[2]

But just how much of a stereotype is the butch/femme lesbian? Throughout the 1940s, 1950s and 1960s in Britain, there certainly were women who were 'butch' and who found partners who could be identified as 'femme'. Jackie Forster, who later founded the magazine and social group, *Sappho*, remembers a visit to the Gateways Club in London in the 1950s. At that time, Gateways was still a mixed bar and attracted both heterosexual and homosexual clientele. She remembers being accosted by a woman who she thought was a man, 'It's so lovely to be here and be yourself' she told her. Later she would be asked if she was 'a boy's girl or a girl's girl'. In the 1950s butch and femme roles were often, though not always, strict. However, there are some doubts as to how much of this behaviour stretched into the bedroom. For many lesbians, butch and femme were a costume and a style but not a sexual behaviour. Jackie Forster herself, found neither of these sexual identities was at all appropriate 'I was never butch or femme, I was just bossy.' It is clear that many other lesbians did not identify in this way, though the prevailing literature of the time, whether it be in lurid paperback novels or even the genteel Georgette Heyer might suggest they ought to. Diana Chapman accepted the image of the lesbian she read in *The Well of Loneliness* on its republication in 1949.

> I was shattered. I thought, 'This is me; this is what it's all about'. . . . But of course it also sold me the idea that all lesbians were masculine and tall and handsome and Stephenish and, of course, I should have looked at myself and realized I wasn't any of these things. I didn't think of lesbians as being ordinary women. I thought, 'There are some women who feel themselves to be men inside, and are therefore attracted to women'. What I didn't ask myself was, 'What about the women on the other side; what are they?'[3]

By the 1960s, lesbians in Britain were beginning to come together not only in gay bars and nightclubs, but in social groups and networks. The publication of the lesbian magazine *Arena 3* and the formation of the social group and magazine *Sappho*, coupled with the creation of other societies like Kenric brought more lesbians together and gave them the opportunity to ask questions about themselves and their identities. Bars like the Gateways in London (by now lesbian only) and the Union Bar, a mixed gay bar in Manchester, still attracted a lesbian clientele that could be divided into butch and femme. The world of the Gateways in London was vividly presented in the film version of *The Killing of Sister George* (released in the late 1960s). Some women have since commented that it felt as if the film brought the curtain down on the era of the 'natty-suited' lesbians as the late 1960s and early 1970s brought more freedom both to women and to lesbians.

Luchia Fitzgerald, a lesbian living in Manchester, remembers her early experiences of the Union Bar in the early 1960s. 'When I first went to the Union, I thought this is not for me, all the women were dressed as men and all the men dressed as women.' She felt that she had to make a choice, either to be a butch or a femme. She chose to be a butch because she did not want to go out with a woman who looked like a man. But she, like many other lesbians, was unhappy with the role – a role that was to continue right into the 1970s. For her, the Union Bar was not just a gay ghetto, it was also a working-class ghetto since middle-class lesbians in Manchester at the time had other ways of meeting, away from this pressure-cooker atmosphere. But the price tag for this ghetto life, with its camaraderie and support, was a strict butch and femme code.

This code brought with it a number of rules. A femme who tried to chat up a butch would be considered 'forward', a butch who started going out with another butch would be publicly ridiculed. Butches were expected to be the bread-winners, but would be considered ponces or pimps if they let their femme keep them. This could be a double-bind: by assuming a strict butch identity, many lesbians found it near impossible to get proper work. In recent years there has been a tendency to suggest that life was easy on the butch, who went out to play darts with the boys while her little wife stayed at home to do the housework. This was not always the case, though it may have been true for some couples. What is clear from many women's stories is that it was not easy to be a butch or a femme.

However, though a woman could present herself as butch, butches did not always take this butchness into bed with them. Maggie Turner, a femme dyke in the 1960s, commented, 'I like sleeping with women because I can be both active and passive. But I remember one really butch woman I slept with, I made love to her and then she turned over and went to sleep – so much for butch.'

The notion that butch lesbians might just be trying to be men was in the minds of many lesbians on the butch/femme bar scene in Manchester at this time. Some butch lesbians may have been using dildos ('Horrible, khaki green they were too' reports one lesbian), but they were often teased – 'So you've had a strapadictomy, have you?' Luchia Fitzgerald remembers butches being teased for wanting to be too male ('Oh, go pull on your clitoris and see if it will grow'), while other butches bragged about having 'stumps'. This kind of banter also makes it clear that lesbians at the time were aware of the roles they were playing.

The writer and academic Elizabeth Wilson, notes the different behaviours between middle-class and working-class dykes.

By the early 1960s, when I started to frequent the Gateways lesbian club in Chelsea, the two modes, the bohemian and traditional butch/femme, coexisted but had a distinct class meaning. The more casual bohemian style was associated with the middle-class teachers, journalists and artists whom my lover and I got to know; strict butch/femme styles were working class. Or that it is how it seemed. On the other hand, two of the then aspiring writers we knew maintained strictly butch roles in their relationships even if they dressed in the casual leather jacket and jeans style that seemed the height of chic.[4]

In America, many writers have written about the 'stone butch', a lesbian who will not let her lover arouse her or touch her sexually and who, therefore, gains her sexual pleasure solely from giving pleasure. 'Stone butch' behaviour has been identified by some lesbian feminists as the worst sort of heterosexist sexual practice. Of course, the gaining of sexual pleasure solely from giving pleasure is not something one automatically associates with male sexual partners. However, the desire not to allow the stone butch decision not to be pleasured has been interpreted by some as 'internalised lesbophobia' as well as 'discomfort at having a female body'.[5]

The experiences of one woman, Rachel, echo this perception:

> There's no doubt that in my early days when I was in love with women . . . there's no doubt about it that I felt in a male role toward them, because I tended to fall in love with women whom I saw as being more feminine than myself, and I certainly didn't want them to pay any attention to the female aspects . . . to my female physical . . . the female bits of my body.[6]

Other women have said to me that though they boasted publicly that they never let their femmes touch them, in secret they actually did. Jackie Forster, remembering a trip to America and the famous Sea Colony Club, was shocked at just how strict butch and femme codes were. Interestingly, she does not believe that butch/femme role-playing in Britain was ever as extreme. It is clear that though some lesbians in Britain may have had an experience of stone butch behaviour, they have not felt it to be a significant sexual identity in itself. A cynic might remark that the recent reclaiming of stone butch behaviour is more about the American movement's desire to reclaim and validate every form of sexual practice and if possible, create a political movement out of it.

It is important to point out that there were, and are, differences in experience of butch and femme role-playing in Britain and America. Through lack of anecdotal information from British lesbians about their experience of butch and femme, some lesbians in the 1980s tended to telescope the American and British experience. In the 1980s and 1990s there was a move to reclaim butch and femme role-playing and incorporate it into lesbian sexual practice. We will see that much of this reclaiming in Britain was based on a very American experience of butch and femme life-style. I believe that lesbians in Britain have largely suppressed the role that the butches and femmes played in the making of our history, and have become rather more obsessed with a sort of feminist cringe factor with regard to their right-off sexual behaviour.

Nor were lesbians themselves happy with butch/femme identifying. In London, as early as 1964, the Minorities Research Group debated whether or not the wearing of male attire to meetings was appropriate. The motion was only narrowly defeated. *Arena 3*, the magazine of the group included a lively debate on the issue. By the early 1970s the debate had begun to change, as new fashions took over the lesbian scene:

Why oh why is it that nine out of ten British lesbians . . .

are about as attractive as cold cabbage? I am overtly
lesbian but nothing on this earth would attract me to a
butch lesbian. I find them as revolting as men. It is
frequently stated that this type of lesbian is in the
minority. I disagree. I've found that if the average lesbian
isn't sporting a shirt and tie, she takes no pride in her
appearance whatsoever.[7]

The response from another *Arena 3* reader is enchanting:

I can assure Miss J. B. that I've met some very attractive,
feminine women – I've been told that I am, too. However,
I think one can be too feminine and attract the wrong
sort – men! This has happened to me and it's very
frustrating when you're longing to meet a nice dominant
(but not masculine) woman.[8]

Some months later there was a rather more anguished plea,
from a correspondent who was finding it all too difficult to
sort out the butches from the femmes:

On a recent trip to Gateways, I had a hard, but fascinating
time deciding t'other from which. Please, dear butches,
stay as you are, as I, for one, am all in favour.[9]

By the end of 1971, an editorial in *Arena 3* re-evaluated
butch and femme. The piece talks about lesbians being at their
butchest before the age of twenty-five, as a result of peer-group
pleasure. It also suggests that femmes, rather than always
encouraging butch behaviour, could in fact de-butch the butch
by getting her to throw away her butch clothes and even seek

out jobs which might demand wearing dresses. But the writer doesn't see the absolute end of the butch lesbian:

> We shall undoubtedly always have with us the 'ultrabutch' but in future we shall notice her more by her attitudes and outlook than by her appearance.

As political debate amongst lesbians grew, whether through the Gay Liberation Front or the Women's Liberation Movement or a local lesbian discussion groups, the butch and femme lesbians came to be seen as a 'bad' thing. Some lesbian GLFers were somewhat disappointed by the 'butch' attitudes of Smithy who ran the Gateways:

> The really sad thing is her negative attitude to her own lesbianism; she came back many times to the statement 'We are abnormal'. I would include as part of her negative attitude and distorted self-image the rigidly sex-defined roles she and her girlfriend feel compelled to play – 'butch' and 'femme', as among the most traditionalist heterosexual couples.[10]

In 1975, *Sappho* magazine's Sextionaire revealed that the majority of lesbians who replied were against butch and femme role-playing. One writer pointed out the complexity of the issue for women of her generation:

> I aspire to avoiding roles but I don't think it's possible for my generation. Is there any part of us that has not been touched by conditioning? The most I expect is to be aware of when it's happening and to swap roles fairly frequently.[11]

If, by the mid-1970s, the butch had had her day, what has been so problematic about the butch and femme identities? Butch/femme is a potent symbol of the extent of our own oppression. It still gives glimpses of the shadow of the sad, sick lesbian, trying and failing to be a man. Indeed, our detractors have made great use of the look of the lesbian as the stick with which to beat us. When lesbians look big, butch and boyish they can easily be written off, not as figures of power or courage, but as figures of fun. The mannish or boyish lesbian remains somehow 'other' and therefore easy to ridicule and dismiss.

But we lesbians can get so hung up about the sexologist's pathologising that it's as if it was solely the butches' or the inverts' fault that we all became oppressed. The threat that lesbianism posed in the late nineteenth and early twentieth century would have been the same whether lesbians smoked cigars and wore men's clothes or not. Indeed, some writers have questioned whether Freud and other sexologists based much of their research on *actual* butch/femme lesbians or simply on what they stereotypically perceived lesbians to be.

Can we really blame Radclyffe Hall (and others who believed in sexological theory) for wanting to find an explanation for her own sexuality? Havelock Ellis could have his 'taint', Freud could have his penis envy, but what none of these 'scientists' could conceive of was that the butch lesbian might actually be seeking not the male body but access into male privilege and power, and thus some sort of credibility. And what could be wrong with wanting male power and privilege when, at the time, there was no such thing as female power and privilege?

But why would women before the Women's Liberation

Movement want to dress and appear butch or femme? Perhaps we should start by looking at how we live as lesbians today. We are schooled in the notion that our lesbianism makes us outsiders. It is only relatively recently that we have begun to see that this 'outsider' status can bring with it a certain freedom. If we live outside society, then, very simply, we don't have to conform to society's mores to survive. Likewise we have also only relatively recently begun to reject the notions of normality versus abnormality that have shaped much of lesbian and gay oppression. We have turned those concepts into something we call 'difference'. We have been able to do this because we have read the books, waived the banners, worn the T-shirts and been to the meetings. There is, now, a lesbian and gay infrastructure to our lives if, when and where we can find it.

But it is really only in the last twenty-five years that we have been able to build and shape that structure, as we have gained both a sense of a politicised lesbian identity and a sense of a tangible lesbian community. Now we can see lesbians on the television, read lesbian novels, see lesbian films, even study lesbianism at university. We can go to lesbian bars and go to lesbian clubs. And we take it for granted that we have our own lesbian role models. For most of this century, however, lesbianism has either remained in the closet or been reviled as unnatural and degenerate. It is not surprising that lesbians created their own strategies for survival.

We have seen how both society's and lesbians' own view of their sexuality was shaped by sexology and we have seen how sexologists helped mould the model of the butch and femme. It is hard not to think of butch and femme in this instant becoming a self-fulfilling prophesy. Today we might accuse the sexologists of creating a stereotype, but bizarrely they also helped shape a role model. Radclyffe Hall was responding to something she found in herself and those in her circle as well as soaking up the ideas of Krafft-Ebing and Havelock Ellis. I am not saying that somehow, suddenly, every lesbian became butch and femme because Radclyffe Hall and Co. had just invented them. Lillian Faderman, in her ground-breaking book *Surpassing the Love of Men*[12] has chronicled what we might style as butch and femme relationships among lesbians much earlier in the nineteenth century (though she points out these are not necessarily sexual). I do believe, however, that Hall and the sexologists did help to make that identity 'official'.

In the 1990s, we can pick and chose from a delicious menu of sexualities. We can be butch, femme, bi, trans-gender, straight or queer. The lesbian in the early part of this century found no such choice on offer. When heterosexuality was not just the norm, but effectively the only apparent sexuality, it seems understandable that women who did seek to spend their lives with other women might replicate the roles they saw played out in 'normal' society around them.

Butch also brings with it instant identification. It has been suggested that lesbians adopted masculinity as a way of signalling their sexual desire for other women.[13] You could equally argue that adopting of masculinity was a way of explaining this desire. The butch costume certainly brought a small freedom – the highly tailored, often severe, skirt suit must have made a wonderful break from the restrictiveness of more feminine attire. It certainly provided the lesbian invert with a clear statement of her 'otherness'. This might result in ridicule, or it might bring another advantage with it.

When the 'mannish lesbian' of the 1920s was caricatured . . . this was because she was potentially a threat to men, claiming male privileges and an active male role not only in the workplace but in the bedroom. Yet when the mannish lesbian dressed in a mannish way she also gained acceptance through giving up her claim to femininity. Provided there were only a few mannish women, they could be accepted as honorary, second-rate, men. For them this may have been a way of surviving.[14]

By the 1960s, the butch costume may have reeked of 'other-ness' from heterosexuality, but it also signalled inclusiveness in the bar scene of the time. Butch costume not only signalled les-bianism, it also brought with it a clear sexual identity. It was a bold advertisement for the sort of woman the butch was seek-ing. For one woman I spoke to, her butch identity was something she put on 'to be a lesbian'. During the day she passed as an ordinary woman, but at night she slicked back her hair, ironed her clothes, polished her shoes and became 'who I am'.

For some, taking on butch or femme roles was a way of sur-vival. The butch lesbian, though often the first to picked on in police raids or to be hassled on the streets, could still be regarded as less of a threat to men and male sexuality as the male perception of the butch lesbian as a woman 'trying to be a man' rendered her both ridiculous and innocuous. Sheila Jeffreys is a trifle more cynical:

What were the advantages and disadvantages for the butch? An advantage must have been the superior status.

Amidst all the hatred directed at lesbians by the straight world, butch lesbians were at least able to feel superior to someone, the femme. But besides this rather limited ego enhancement there were, according to most accounts, serious disadvantages.[15]

The most serious disadvantage these days is the disapproval of sanctimonious lesbians. Sheila Jeffreys, in a not unusual political stance, wants it both ways. She talks later in the same article of role-playing as 'the enforced survival tactics of a lesbian community', but she still reserves the right to patronise at least one of its victims.

The above quote neatly takes us to the main criticism that many lesbians have made regarding women who take on butch or femme identities. For them, both butches and femmes are really consorting with the enemy. Rather than challenging the system they are, in effect, conspiring with it. The butch is the easier target, of course. Butches are simply aping heterosexuality, taking the worst attributes of men – violence, drinking, disdain for women – and making it all their own. Thus butches become an integral part of the system that oppresses women everywhere. Femmes are the victims of this male-identified behaviour, but they are also guilty themselves. They bob merrily between homosexuality and heterosexuality, wherever and whenever it suits them. They allow themselves to play at being a heterosexual woman and worse still, choose to play it with a pseudo-man.

Any discussion of butch and femme role-playing in Britain hits a problem. Where are the femmes? Much of the argument in the 1980s about butch and femme role-playing was based on American research and American experience. Now, we all know that British lesbians can't do anything without making sure the Americans did it first. But we have already seen how some British lesbians have questioned the concept of stone butch. The femme voice in Britain has stayed largely silent. I can remember discussions where this silence was taken as proof positive of just how oppressed the poor femmes must be. Other theories concluded that most femmes must have crawled guiltily back to heterosexuality. The great irony is, of course, that it is much easier to subsume the butch lesbian identity into the right-on lesbian environment. For much of the 1980s, the lipstick lesbian (yesterday's femme) was a powerful symbol of what the lesbian must not be, feeble, feminine, to be taken at the whim of the male. It is very hard to imagine that a British femme lesbian would ever have the courage to champion her experience in the way that activists like Joan Nestle or Amber Hollinbaugh have done in the States.

When I came out in the early 1980s I came out into a world of egalitarian relationships and endless self-policing. In the circles I moved in at the time there was much concern about butch behaviour. Butch behaviour might mean arguing too aggressively in a meeting, wearing the wrong sort of clothes or chatting up women in bars; it could be defined as any behaviour that might be in the least bit male. All this was, of course, highly subjective.

In the late 1980s, the lesbian feminist journal *Gossip* ran a number of features about butch and femme and its place in the lesbian community and in lesbian politics at the time. Anna Livia looked at butch behaviour and showed some of the confusion that women felt then at the notion of butch or femme. What did butch and femme really mean and what was its significance for the 1980s lesbian? More confusing was the fact that some lesbians just looked more butch than others. This conflation of butchness with maleness could be distressing and Livia has an interesting insight into the problem:

> the dykes I know who are often taken for men do not like it, feel angry, miserable, confused, guilty. They are not trying to pass as men. The hurtful confusion of butch with male is made worse by the use of the terms 'role' and 'role-playing'. If you say 'role-playing' in a lesbian context, everyone thinks of butch and femme, implying that dykes who think of themselves as one or the other are only playing a game, that they are performing a part in a play, therefore that costume and lines are predetermined, that their butch characteristics are not their own, but somehow unreal, inauthentic. This seems to me to be very close to the heterosexual mode of thought which perceives lesbianism as a brief rebellion, a phase, and accepts lesbian relationships of twenty or thirty years only insofar as these echo heterosexual relations and which casts the dykes they really cannot recuperate in a predatory wolf stereotype.[16]

Livia's essay hints that she at least believes in a sort of natural butchness in certain lesbians. At the same time she reminds us of how standards of butchness and femmeness could vary between lesbian social groupings. This was not always a source of lesbian feminist politicking but also a bit of lesbian fun. Yet there was also a negative side to the day-to-day negotiations of behaving or looking butch (being called 'son' or 'mate'), or behaving femme (asking the AA to help change a tyre), which could either bring on a little feminist guilt or lesbian confusion . . .

However, the late 1980s saw women both theorising and politicising again about the concepts of butch and femme and incorporating these concepts into their lives and sex lives. In 1988 Sheba published Joan Nestle's collection of essays and fiction *A Restricted Country*. At the same time, a number of other American lesbians began reclaiming and celebrating their experiences of butch/femme role-playing and a major piece of research into one butch/femme community was published. Nestle's book is both empowering and inspirational, and within it is a powerful reclamation of the butch/femme life-style, and most particularly the femme. She uses a historical perspective taken from her own experience to question the perceived 'passivity' of the femme and her victim status. It is this mixture of personal, historical and political that gives *A Restricted Country* its undoubted power.

Joan Nestle was also a speaker at the 1982 Barnard Conference on sexuality and feminism where she gave a powerful definition of what butch/femme (fem) meant as she experienced it.

> For many years now, I have been trying to figure out how to explain the special nature of butch/fem relationships to feminists and lesbian feminists who consider butch-fem a reproduction of heterosexual models and therefore dismiss both lesbian communities of the past and of the present that assert this style . . . Living a butch-fem life was not an intellectual exercise; it was not a set of theories . . . In the most basic terms, butch-fem means a way of looking, loving, and living that can be expressed by individuals, couples or a community. In the past, the butch has been labelled too simplistically the masculine partner and the

fem her feminine counterpart. This labelling forgets two women who have developed their styles for specific erotic, emotional, and social reasons. Butch-fem relationships, as I experienced them, were complex erotic and social statements, not phoney heterosexual replicas.[17]

But is there such a thing as a truly butch or femme lesbian? So far we have mainly talked about butch and femme as role-playing, as a dynamic that a lesbian might choose, for what ever reason, by which to live her life. This takes for granted the notion that butch and femme are socially constructed. Butch and femme, to many of the women living those dynamics at the time, could be a role that society forced on her, a safe space where she might live her life, a way to survive in a hostile, heterosexual environment. It is hard not to see these experiences as constructed by the forces of society at the time.

In the late 1980s and early 1990s, some lesbians, while reclaiming butch and femme, began to suggest that this identity might be innate. The notion that one could be literally born butch or born femme is as complex and as dangerous a point of discussion as that we are born lesbian or heterosexual. Lesbian feminists have pointed out that returning to the notions of an innate lesbian sexuality brings us dangerously back within the realms of sexology and the medicalisation of homosexuality. Other writers have wondered whether lesbians should not actively explore these issues as a key to understanding our sexuality better.

There has been relatively little attempt to incorporate the complexities of butch and femme roles into a radical feminist framework in a way that could recognise the courage of the butch (and femme) lesbians of the early decades of this century and which might provide a political perspective on their importance to lesbian history and identities. To refuse to acknowledge the (continuing) existence of butch and femme roles, to avoid discussion of their meaning, is to discount and dismiss the survival strategies of many of our lesbian sisters and foresisters. Until the experience of 'butch' and 'femme' lesbians is acknowledged, accepted and analyzed with as much clarity as is the experience of the heterosexual woman, both they and feminism will be the poorer.[18]

Our lesbian sex wars have made this analysis very difficult. Butch/femme and role-playing have become deeply loaded terms for us. They tell not about our history as lesbians but about whether or not we can gain acceptance into one of the two lesbian camps: that which abhors those practices and finds them male-identified and that which comes from a sex radical agenda which finds the lesbian feminist approach unacceptable. We focus too easily on the idea of butch/femme as something we do in the bedroom and if lesbian feminism has been guilty of ignoring the complexities of butch/femme then, indeed, so have the so-called sex radicals. Writers like Joan Nestle have tried to explore this difficult area and it is sad to see their work both simplified and trivialised.

In Britain, we have scarcely come to terms with butch/femme role-playing as part of our lesbian history. Indeed, I believe that there is still a collective lesbian embarrassment about our role-playing foremothers and it is time we began to recognise their part in creating our lesbian history. However, modern discussions of butch/femme have tended to concentrate on role-playing as a sexual practice rather than as an aspect of our lesbian history. There is a danger that when the late 1980s and 1990s reclamations of butch/femme ignore the historical context of that role-playing, it becomes all too easily conflated with SM. If SM is an exchange of power between two sexual partners, then role-playing can be seen as a clear display of that power. We have looked at how, historically, this display of power could be used as a survival strategy, as a way of signalling desire or simply as a disguise. If we reduce butch/femme simply to the bedroom, we not only risk denying, or at the very least trivialising, our own history and experience but also turning butch/femme into nothing more than SM behaviour. It is no coincidence then, that when butch/femme was reduced simply to sexual practice, it became a major part of the lesbian sex wars.

But let's remember that even in the lesbian feminist heyday, the butch/femme lesbian never completely went away. You can still find her in certain clubs, bars or walking down the street. Many of these women have never been touched by the brouhaha of political debate, they have neither been 'reclaimed' nor 'reconstructed', they find their own ways of living and loving without a 'lesbian community' or a political ideology. Among politically sussed 1990s lesbians, these women often raise a condescending smile. They still have the power to make us feel uncomfortable and they still raise difficult questions about our lesbian sexuality. I wonder what mysteries go on behind their bedroom doors?

Knowing What's Good For Us

Lesbian feminism and the politicising of lesbian sex

In the late 1980s, in certain circles, if you asked what a lesbian feminist was, you would probably be told that she was uniformly patronising, judgemental and totally humourless. A lesbian feminist would tell everyone what to do but would never do it herself. She probably didn't do sex and if she did she probably didn't enjoy it much. A lesbian feminist was the dinosaur of the dyke movement. If ever there was a group of women who have been misunderstood and misrepresented, it is the lesbian feminists. In the lesbian sex wars they have become the ultimate bad girls. By questioning the politics of the lesbian bedroom and by questioning certain sexual practices, they themselves have become the oppressors. Never mind oppressive heterosexuality, never mind such outdated concepts as patriarchal supremacy, it seems that these days it is the lesbian feminist who really threatens lesbian freedom. But why have lesbian feminists recently got such a bad press from the lesbian community? And why did their politics lay the ground for the lesbian sex wars'

Lesbian feminism sprung out of the movement for the liberation of women which began in the 1970s. In Britain the

Women's Liberation Movement changed how women regarded both themselves and their position in society. Patriarchal assumptions were challenged as women's relationships with men were put under the microscope. For lesbians, the Women's Liberation Movement signalled their inclusion in a new vision of women's place in the world.

In its beginnings, the WLM embraced a wide range of women with a wide range of different political ideologies. Whether you were a socialist feminist or a radical feminist you could still march under the banner of sisterhood. However, as the movement progressed through the 1970s, there was antagonism about the root cause of women's oppression. Radical feminists, or revolutionary feminists, believed that women's oppression was a direct result of male power, while other feminist groupings questioned the simplicity of this approach, believing that you could not easily dismiss issues like class or capitalism from the causes of women's oppression.

Added to this was a growing antagonism between lesbians and heterosexual women within the movement.

The public reaction to the reawakening of feminism was to dismiss us all as bra-burning lesbians. The reaction of WLM was strenuously to deny this 'insult'. Heterosexual feminists argued that we had to be taken seriously as women, and if the media got away with the label of lesbians, then 'the women out there' would be alienated . . . As the seventies wore on the numbers of lesbians in the WLM increased dramatically, the rumbles of discontent turned into roars. Lesbians put their weight behind issues such as child-care, abortion, race, battered wives and rape. In return we wanted the skeleton of sexuality wrenched from the closet and flesh put on its bones.[1]

A woman's right to define her sexuality did become the seventh demand of the WLM, but heterosexual women within the movement began to challenge what they perceived as the holier-than-thou attitudes of lesbians within the movement. Separatists like Janet Dixon who, inspired by a radical feminist analysis, had chosen to sever themselves totally from men, were particularly threatening to straight feminists who felt their life-styles to be judged and condemned. As the 1970s progressed, views became more entrenched and antagonisms ran high, and the Womens Liberation Movement effectively broke apart after its last conference in Birmingham in 1978.

But that was not the end of lesbian and feminist activism. Lesbians still met together in discussion groups, consciousness raising groups and in women-only spaces; they were still involved in Rape Crisis, Women's Aid, Women's book shops, Women's newsletters and there was still a vigorous women's network. By the early 1980s, many women had begun to define themselves as both lesbians and lesbian feminists. In 1979 the Leeds Revolutionary Feminists circulated a pamphlet called *Political Lesbianism: The Case Against Heterosexuality*. Defining a 'political lesbian as a woman-identified woman who does not fuck men', the pamphlet describes lesbianism as a 'necessary political choice, part of the tactics of our struggle, not a passport to happiness'. For heterosexual women the message of the Leeds Revolutionary Feminists was clear:

Men are the enemy. Heterosexual women are collaborators with the enemy. All the good work that our heterosexual sisters do for women is undermined by the counter-revolutionary activity they engage in with men.[2]

This rather doctrinaire approach not only angered some heterosexual feminists, but it made some lesbians distinctly uncomfortable too. Strangely, when the Leeds women talked about women-identified women, they also made it clear that political lesbianism did not mean 'compulsory sexual activity with women'. This may have been a method of calming the fluttering nerves of some heterosexual women but it was to have repercussions on how political lesbianism and lesbian feminism were to be regarded by lesbians in the future.

Lesbian feminism sees the oppression of women through heterosexuality as central to male power. Lesbian feminists questioned male supremacy and showed how male violence and the use of male power lay at the heart of women's oppression. Women, by choosing to be 'women identified', and to concentrate their energies and attentions solely on each other could challenge, and indeed destabilise, male power. If feminism was the theory, then lesbianism logically had to be the practice. Likewise, lesbian feminism stressed the old adage that the 'personal had to be political', thus every aspect of a woman's life was put under scrutiny to see how it could be a part of the lesbian feminist vision.

Nowhere is the ethos behind this brand of feminism more clearly articulated than in Adrienne Rich's essay 'Compulsory Heterosexuality and Lesbian Existence'. Rich argues that heterosexuality is a 'political institution' that has overpowered women and denied them freedom and independence from men.

. . . when we look hard and clearly at the extent and

elaboration of measures designed to keep women within a
male sexual purlieu, it becomes an inescapable question
whether the issue we have to address as feminists is not
simple 'gender inequality', nor the domination of culture
by males, nor mere 'taboos against homosexuality', but
the enforcement of heterosexuality for women as a means
of assuring male right of physical, economical, and
emotional access. One of many means of enforcement is,
of course, the rendering invisible of the lesbian possibility,
an engulfed continent which rises fragmentedly to view
from time to time only to become submerged again.[3]

Rich then goes on to discuss what she considers to be the
'lesbian continuum' – that range of women-identified experience that need not necessarily include sex with other women.
The lesbian continuum can include all sorts of experiences
including the 'sharing of a rich inner life, 'bonding against
male tyranny, the 'giving and receiving of practical and political support' and presumably giving her your last Rolo. It is
this part of Rich's analysis that has raised questions with many
lesbians. By pulling together a range of not specifically lesbian experiences and calling them lesbian, she effectively
de-lesbians the lesbian and turns her into a sort of touchy/feely
Everywoman. This might be an effective strategy for integrat-
ing non-lesbian women in the lesbian feminist world view (i.e.
by making them non-practising lesbians), but it does not really
give those lesbians who actively, loudly and proudly embrace
their lesbianism (and that of other people's) much of a look-in.
Bizarrely, Rich argues for the lesbian's place in history and
her place in challenging heterosexuality, only to lose her in
mists of women-identified experience.

The other great lesbian feminist visionary of the early 1980s was Mary Daly. In such books as *Gyn/Ecology*[4] and *Pure Lust*[5] Daly lays down a challenge to male power, or the 'Cockocracy' as she describes it. She demonstrates how language has been used to suppress women's voices and women's energy. She shows how language has been used to replace the naturally female order of the world with patriarchal voice and power. Lesbians within this context are the witches, the women who are outside male society and therefore create the greatest threat to that society. Lesbians, or as she calls them 'women-touching women', also share an unconscious understanding and communication with the 'mother' nature. Personally, I have always found this rather difficult to stomach. However, at a time in the early 1980s when we still felt greatly threatened by nuclear proliferation, Daly's work struck a powerful chord. The nuclear arsenal was easily constructed as male and as a dangerous symbol of patriarchial power; unchallenged it would destroy the world. Women could, in their relationship with nature, overturn this power. It is no coincidence that lesbians, who provided the back-bone of protest at Greenham Common, used the imagery of nature, spiders' webs, rainbows as powerful symbols of women's natural power.

Many lesbians in the late 1970s and early 1980s were greatly sustained by lesbian feminism. Lesbians were not only part of a powerful political movement but they were leading from the front. Heterosexual men might nervously make jokes about hairy-legged lesbians but it was clear that they felt threatened and attacked. Most importantly of all, lesbianism had been rescued from the clutches of the sexologists and radically redefined. The Women's Liberation Movement gave lesbians the chance to meet other lesbians, to form vital networks, to set up conferences and discussion groups. For many lesbians it was also a safe space where women could talk about their histories and their experiences and talk openly about their sexuality, for many for the first time. There were, indeed, women who 'came to lesbianism through the feminist movement'.

And the binding of feminism with lesbianism was extremely useful. For one lesbian living in Edinburgh, the politics of the time were 'very much about seeing someone as a whole person in the context of the society around them. It was about trying to validate a lesbian's life in every aspect of her life, because straight society only defines you by who you have sex with.' Indeed, lesbian feminism made it clear that lesbianism did not exist in a vacuum, that lesbians' lives were affected by the politics of the society around them. At the same time, many lesbians needed to have both their lives and their experiences validated, after all, many lesbians were still facing discrimination in their workplaces and from their families. At the same time as creating a political context for women, lesbian feminism also continued to nurture and support many lesbians. In a 1990s world that is tied up in notions of individualism and independence, it is easy to dismiss the collectivism and sense of community that a shared politics brought to women at the time.

Yet the most damning criticism lesbian feminists have faced over the last ten years is that they are not only anti-sex but are also some sort of lesbian sex-police. The idea that lesbian feminists policed lesbian sexuality has been greeted with great surprise by some of the women I have talked to. They have pointed out that there was never a Lesbian Feminist Ten Commandments, the first of which would have been 'Thou shalt not enjoy lesbian sex'. What there was, they say, was discussion about a number of different issues, from objectification, to non-monogamy and penetration. There was also, amongst this discussion, a certain amount of trial and error. Opinions about these issues might also vary quite considerably from group to group. As one woman put it, 'In Leeds, ten years ago, you couldn't do anything apart from set yourself on fire and throw yourself at a sex shop.' The same behaviours were not necessarily being replicated in London, Bristol or Edinburgh. Yet other women do feel that lesbian feminism could be doctrinaire and limiting, a blanket rejection of butch/femme for example, which left many women feeling that the complexity of the issue had never been fully explored.

There was much discussion among lesbian feminists about non-monogamy and its role in lesbian relationships. Because lesbian feminism did not separate personal life from the political, it was felt important to put women's relationships, both with men and with women, under the microscope. Monogamy was demanded of women in heterosexual relationships and it could be seen to be one of the ways in which patriarchy controlled women's freedom within a relationship. It was felt that lesbians who were monogamous were therefore aping heterosexuality and heterosexual oppression. Non-monogamy was, therefore, a challenge to patriarchal assumptions about female sexuality. It was also felt that women could have a number of different relationships with women while avoiding the jealousy and possessiveness that could mar monogamous relationships. Thus, women could create positive blueprints for their sexuality and their sexual behaviour.

However, for many lesbians, the practice of non-monogamy was often more difficult than the theory. Penny Wallace, a lesbian now living in Newcastle, remembers her brushes with non-monogamy.

> My partner's non-monogamy led to problems, even
> though she was clear from the beginning that she wanted
> to be non-monogamous. Intellectually, I thought it was an
> interesting concept, but intellectual theory is different
> from being faced with reality. I discovered that non-
> monogamy is fine when you are doing it, but very different
> when your partner is doing it. I became jealous and
> though I tried to explore what I was jealous of, it made
> very little difference.

While some women could see the many advantages that
non-monogamy could bring to lesbian relationships, they still
admit that they saw very few working in practice. For true
non-monogamy to work, each partner needed honesty, clarity
and the time to talk through and acknowledge problems. This
could be very good for a relationship but at the same time,
utterly exhausting. It was also suggested that women could
have a 'primary' partner while at the same time having sexual
relationships with other 'lesser' partners. In an ideal world, the
'primary' partner would have no need to feel jealous and the
other partners would know exactly where they stood. Many
women could see the appeal of this rigorous approach to form-
ing relationships, but again it was hard to make them work.
This was because, despite all the honesty and the clarity, the
'primary' partner did feel jealous and the 'secondary' partner
felt used or left out. The problem with all this was, of course,
that non-monogamy for many women was incompatible with
love. Whilst partnerships were seen as a sound alternative to
the idea of love, with all its heterosexist Mills and Boon

trappings, it was very difficult to keep complex emotions out of lesbian relationships. You cannot shape complex emotions like love and fit them comfortably within political parameters.

For some lesbians, the lesbian feminist espousal of non-monogamy was also an opportunity to have a really good time. One woman puts it rather succinctly: 'Any one can fuck around – you don't have to call it non-monogamy – it's just fucking around.' Julie Bindel, a lesbian feminist activist, admits that at one point she had four lovers. 'I refused to have just one because I said it would be exclusive and other sorts of crap. I just treated women like shit under the umbrella of good politics. I don't think it's sexy to behave badly. I used to, but that was my own choice, it was not dictated to me by my lesbian feminist betters.' But she goes on to add that non-monogamy did challenge the old heterosexual-style attitudes like 'she's my bird' or 'she's my bit on the side'. The other problem was also, that by being so scrupulously honest about your other lovers or your primary partner, you were taking all the fun out of non-monogamy and sacrificing spontaneity.

It is ironic to think it was the lesbian feminists who most strongly espoused the notion of non-monogamy in lesbian relationships. Our relationships, even in the 1990s, are still posited around romantic notions of faithfulness and long-term love. Some of us have criticised the nesting instinct of the average lesbian. We forget that formal couple relationships provide us with a stability that our relationships with the outside world sometimes lack. In the mid-1990s, the pressure to be in couple relationships remains very strong. The woman who is not afraid to have lots of sexual partners still elicits lots of comment. In the 1970s and early 1980s, the lesbian feminist movement itself provided an important stability for many lesbians either coming out or already out on the scene. The scene could be a very secure and safe environment in which to play around with new ideas about how we might structure our relationships.

Another issue that caused discussion amongst lesbian feminists was the politics of 'fancying'.

> Fancying was, and is, seen, by many as objectifying, as based on rules about physical perfection which were deeply discriminatory, even sometimes racist and ableist, and as reflecting a construction of sexuality which was hostile to women's interests. It was felt that a simple and learned physical urge towards a stranger was not a good way to begin relationships. Not all lesbians felt that they had overcome, or wanted to overcome, the learned sexual practice of 'fancying' but there was great good will and commitment to discussing these ideas.[6]

This all sounds rather sweet, but there is nothing wrong with the notion of looking deeper at a person than simple physical attractiveness. It also validated the notion that you could be intimate with someone before you went to bed with them. And, as Julie Bindel points out, thinking about how you objectify women could indeed challenge your own preconceptions of who you might or might not be attracted to. But some women have pointed out that it is very hard not to objectify the women around you. 'I could go and have a drink in a bar, then I would look round and think "Oh, my god, am I objectifying anyone?"'

Penny Wallace also felt that there was quite a difference between 'fancying' someone and simply being 'attracted'. 'I don't separate physical and emotional attraction. Intellectually I can, but it has never happened to me. I don't think it is just socialisation, but I really have to have both.' Another lesbian now living in Bradford never had much of a problem around 'fancying'. She was quite happy to chat women up in bars and though some women did criticise her and warn her about this 'male' behaviour, she went ahead and did it anyway.

There was also some question about whether lesbian sex should include any element of penetration. It is often said that all lesbian feminists were fundamentally opposed to penetration. Certainly the use of dildos and vibrators was questioned and condemned as being a clear attempt to mimic heterosexual sex, but digital penetration was still a part of many lesbians' love-making. For other women, penetration in any form was absolutely unacceptable. The notion of what was unacceptable and acceptable could vary from group to group. One woman I know was roundly condemned for asking her partner to have penetrative sex with her. It was not just her partner's consternation that was upsetting but the fact that she then related this *faux pas* to all her lesbian cronies. Other groups of women were able to talk quite openly about their enjoyment of penetration, in previous heterosexual relationships and in current lesbian ones.

Lesbian feminism encouraged women to be open about their sexual desires but in a very limited way. There was a sense in which women were encouraged to tell their partners what they wanted in their love-making and what they enjoyed. Within this there were guide-lines about what was unacceptable or acceptable, but these were often left unspoken. Thus, lesbian sex could be something of a minefield for the politically uninitiated. Many women's first experience of lesbian sex could be awkward and intimidating. For one woman 'lesbian sex was something totally new, it was treated as something mystical and mysterious. My lover seemed to expect that I would know exactly what to do, instinctively. She seemed too embarrassed to actually show me or tell me herself.' This is an experience that many other women I have spoken to recognise. There almost seems to be an expectation that if once you come out as a lesbian, you will automatically understand all the sexual mechanics. The romantic-fiction format, that lesbian sex was really about 'caressing each other's wetness' was not very much help.

For many women, however, the chance to talk about what they wanted from sex was incredibly empowering and a real change from what they had been used to from their male partners. Yet others found this process of negotiation rather clinical and 'unsexy'. The whole notion of discussing sex with your partner could become exhausting or slightly ridiculous. A lesbian I know, after sex with a new partner, was asked if she would like to 'evaluate the experience'. Yet, although there was this encouragement of discussion, many lesbians found it very hard. Women have been very successfully socialised not to talk about their sexual feelings and their sexual desires, and feminism, while encouraging *perestroika* with your partner, did not find a language of sex that moved beyond the idealised notion that sex should be 'mutual', 'equal' and an expression of your 'woman-centredness'. Though you can encourage women to talk about what they want, that doesn't automatically mean they will tell you what they *don't* want. Lesbian sex remained an intensely private business based on a series of collective ideals. Within this, it was often difficult for women who, for whatever reason, were not enjoying sex to have an outlet for their feelings. To talk about sex in a way that was not demeaning to your partner, or in some way aped heterosexist language, was intensely difficult. One woman found it impossible to talk about the fact that she was not reaching orgasm in her love-making. Were orgasms patriarchal? Could you get orgasms from lesbian sex, anyway?

For some women, the constant reinforcement of the message that women's relationships with women would be based on 'caring', 'sharing' and 'mutual support' did not hide the fact that their relationships were none of those things. Lesbianism became idealised as the perfect sort of relationship where a woman would never have to worry about pain or a broken heart. We have already seen how non-monogamy could be used by some women as an excuse for a good time. When your lover was doing the politically correct thing, it could be very hard to admit that you found this distressing. It is always hard to talk about what is going wrong in a relationship, but it is even more difficult when that relationship is being held up as an ideal model. In this climate women also found it very hard to talk about the fact that they had experienced violence in their relationships with other women or to talk about sexual behaviours that they found difficult. For some women, the idea that their partner might actively seek to be non-monogamous was deeply distressing and disempowering, it was often difficult to admit to these feelings when non-monogamy was held up as the right model to follow.

Separatism also influenced how women regarded sex and sexuality. Separatism had been a part of lesbian politics from early in the WLM. For lesbian separatists, it was not enough to question patriarchal views, a total separation from men was the only way to live a truly feminist existence. Though you could be a separatist and a lesbian feminist, you did not have to be a separatist to be a lesbian feminist. Separatism, as an attempt to create that lesbian utopia, was particularly stringent at removing all vestiges of male-identified behaviour from the lesbian psyche. Some separatists chose celibacy (as indeed did other women) as a way of challenging the heterosexist and patriarchal structure of relationships which relied on the use of power of one person over another. Other separatists believed that non-monogamy was essential to lesbian relationships and that sex was an expression of collectiveness and connectedness. It wasn't that separatist lesbians believed anything fundamentally different from their lesbian sisters, they just lived their politics with an extraordinary rigour. This separatist energy was undoubtedly an influence in the wider lesbian feminist arena. Many non-separatist lesbians found this rather unsettling, they felt judged and left wanting, while separatists themselves became frustrated by their sisters' failure to grasp the mettle.

I do not wish to attack the whole concept of separatism as other lesbians have done, but there were times when separatism could influence a rather worrying extremism. One woman was criticised for touching her lover's breasts because this was deemed to be objectification. It is this rather extreme approach that has created some of the ammunition that later commentators, both lesbian and heterosexual, have used to attack lesbian feminism. This is an awkward argument since you can take any action, place it out of its political context and make a mockery of it. Likewise, feminism's success can often be most accurately measured by the anger and ridicule it engenders. But the great weakness of separatism was that it could never really address the problem of men in any meaningful way, unless you advocated 'sending all men to the moon' (once suggested in all seriousness at a lesbian discussion group), or wholesale genocide. Nor was it really possible to imagine that all women could one day live in total separation.

Many more lesbians did connect their lesbianism and feminism to the natural, female world. Some separatist lesbian groups moved to rural areas where they could more easily commune with mother nature. Not all lesbians were as enthusiastic about the ecological feminism that writers like Mary Daly espoused. Heather Savage, a lesbian in Edinburgh, sums it up like this: 'I hated all the ecology shit, I never felt that I could communicate with trees, or that I had an elemental connection with my cat. Though I could see that women were oppressed by patriarchy, I did not see that automatically meant they should commune with nature. It was this weird attitude that "All women are trees, all women are the wind, all women are beautiful and all men are bastards."' This linking of women with nature was vital to the creation of the Women's Peace Movement and particularly to the setting-up of the protest about nuclear armament at Greenham Common. Many, many lesbians went to Greenham and it became an extraordinarily potent symbol of women's power and unity in the face of male aggression. Like the early days of the WLM, Greenham gave many women a safe space where they could explore their lesbianism. The camp at Green Gate became a completely separatist environment. What Greenham showed, for many lesbians, was that you could link ideas of separatism, ecology and political lesbianism into a coherent whole. However, once the missiles were removed from the equation, these ideas quickly lost their focus.

For journalist Cherry Smyth, who came out in the early

1980s through the Peace Movement, lesbian sex was both nurturing and supportive but also strangely limiting. It was not possible to talk about eroticism or fantasy and what role they had played, or could play, in your sex life because such notions were dangerously heterosexist and patriarchal. She believes there 'was an incredible insecurity about lesbian sexuality, based on a need to consolidate a very closed lesbian culture'. Certainly, it is remarkably difficult to integrate fully the demands of a political ideology into your personal life. This is why lesbian feminism placed so much emphasis on the collective energies of women as a way of ensuring that the message of lesbian feminism could be regularly reinforced. This was often made easier by the fact that many women involved in lesbian feminist politics were working for organisations like Women's Aid or Rape Crisis that were founded on strong feminist principles.

Lesbian feminism and political lesbianism had initially been created as a way to bring all women, gay or straight, into a political movement that could challenge the power of patriarchy through the collective power of women's energy. Many women did come out as a result of this and espoused lesbian feminism, but it was also very clear that many other women drifted away from this rather limiting feminist view. At this point, I believe, lesbian feminism, rather than keeping its gaze upon the wider world, turned that gaze upon itself. It was not clear whether lesbian feminism had become a lesbian utopia or a lesbian bunker. Either way, there was a need to 'consolidate' that particular view of lesbianism and, if necessary, protect it. 'Heterosexist behaviour', a catch-all phrase that could be used to describe any behaviour that might be considered dangerous or unacceptable, became a threat to the lesbian feminist ideal.

There were other confusions too. If you were a feminist and a lesbian, did you have to be a lesbian feminist? In the early 1980s, lesbian feminism was probably the most dominant lesbian ideology and the boundaries between lesbian feminism and feminism itself were rather unclear. So much so that the voice of lesbian feminism was often deemed by lesbian feminists to be the only voice of feminism. This is crucial to the idea of lesbian sex wars. When lesbian feminists took upon themselves the sole mantle of feminism, it meant that other views, other ideas and other sexual practices became both threatening and unacceptable.

Not surprisingly, bisexuality was considered to be totally unacceptable in a lesbian feminist environment. But, for the not insignificant group of women who defined themselves as bisexual, this attitude was both hurtful and excluding. They felt it was possible to be both a feminist and a bisexual. For lesbian feminists, the rejection of men was a vital part of being a lesbian feminist – those who continued to have sexual contact with men, or did not rule out the possibility of having sex with men, were still playing by men's rules. But the debates around bisexuality which continued throughout the 1980s were often angry and antagonistic. Bisexuals pointed out that not all lesbian relationships were perfect and that women often behaved as badly as men did. Lesbians countered that bisexuals were 'just sitting on the fence . . . using lesbianism and running back to heterosexuality when it suited them' and even that they were 'just going through a phase'. Many bisexuals felt that though the debates were supposed to be political, they were actually being exposed to a tremendous amount of personal attack. Many felt their lives and ideas were attacked in a manner that was intrusive and insensitive. Though some women argued that bisexuality could be included in a lesbian feminist politics, it was clear that bisexuality posed more of a personal threat than a political one.

The condemnation of bisexuality by both lesbians and lesbian feminists brings up the whole issue of lesbian insecurity around sexuality. When straight bigots say that if everybody was gay there would be no more human race, they are not just being crass but are also revealing their own insecurity. There must be something really good about homosexual sex – and therefore something really lacking in heterosexual sex – for them to believe that everybody is going to want to do it. Likewise, a similar insecurity is at play when lesbians believe that the mere existence of a few bisexual women or a few women eroticising sex are going to threaten lesbianism so completely. The difference is that whereas heterosexuality was an ancient construction, the construction of lesbianism in the 1970s and 1980s was a very new one. Lesbians still faced a tremendous amount of ridicule, discrimination and even violence as a result of their sexuality. The fear that large numbers of women might turn back to men was understandable. It is also natural under such circumstances, that lesbians would want to protect all they had fought for. For many lesbians, even in the queer 1990s, the thought of being abandoned by your partner for a man is very different to being abandoned for another woman: it is a judgement both on one's self and one's sexuality. In an earlier chapter we looked at the need for lesbians to create definitions for themselves and their sexuality. Lesbian feminism created a very clear definition of what lesbianism should and should not be, but it left no room for change, development or question.

While lesbian feminism had provided many women with a

strong sense of themselves and their sexuality, there were still those women who did not believe their sexuality was directly rooted in the feminist movements of the 1970s and early 1980s.

> The Women's Liberation Movement has taken lesbianism and joined it to itself in theory and practice so that in some explanations the justification for lesbianism was feminism and vice versa. In the first flush of our enthusiasm for feminism we tended to validate, or at the very least heavily criticise, our history and construction. As the debate around sex and sexuality comes again in the Women's Liberation Movement I find that I have not ordered my world through 'rage against men'. In certain crucial areas my view and construction of my own lesbianism is quite different from that of many women who came to it through feminism.[7]

One of the major criticisms of the lesbian feminist vision of lesbianism was that it actually down-played, and even deval-ued, lesbian experience. The definition of a lesbian as being someone 'who did not fuck men' was both negative and hardly a reflection of the diversity of the lesbian world. The all-encompassing notion of the woman-identified woman actually left the lesbian with little or no status. In what was to become one of the ground-breaking essays in considering the influence of lesbian feminism, Wendy Clark adds,

> If lesbians continue to allow the category 'lesbian' to be the same as 'women', then we deny ourselves and allow only a continuing existence as another social category

with different and distinctly gendered limits. But the lesbian struggle for self-definition and autonomy has been in process for a long time. If we want further to strengthen and develop this self-definition and autonomy we have to circumvent this present impasse in which lesbianism finds itself engulfed by feminism. The geography of both countries is complicated and unique, and the boundaries only overlap in places.[8]

As the 1980s progressed, more and more lesbians sought out this self-definition. As lesbians began to explore new politics and new pleasures, the collectivist power of lesbian feminism began to waver. For a brief time in the late 1970s and early 1980s it was possible to believe that lesbian was just another word for woman and woman just another word for lesbian. But as the world changed in the Thatcher years it became clear that just as lesbian feminism had said no woman existed in a vacuum, neither did lesbian feminism. As collectivism gave way to individualism it became less and less easy for lesbian feminists to get their voices heard. As a result, I believe, the lesbian feminist message has often been exaggerated or distorted, but at the same time that message became increasingly irrelevent and anachronistic.

Were lesbian feminists really anti-sex? One woman I met strongly refutes this accusation, saying, 'Coming out as a lesbian was throwing sex in straight society's face. It was standing up to the world and saying this is what we do and this what we are. I feel pissed off that a lot of work that we did, the energy we put into looking at the politics of being alive as a lesbian and fighting for our rights and recognition, is taken for granted by many dykes today.' What lesbian feminism tried to do was put sex into a political context. By believing that the personal had to be political, it was clear that sex itself couldn't exist in isolation, nor could it be the only defining part of one's lesbian feminist identity.

> Lesbianism to a feminist is much more than just a question of sex. It's a question of life-style; it's a question of sexual politics. It's much wider than the sexual act.
>
> The important thing about being a lesbian is not the sexual act itself. It's the self-definition in that way as a woman-identified woman, and the commitment to women.[9]

Lesbian feminism as a political ideology has a major flaw: its continual emphasis on challenging patriarchal power by focusing women's energy lets patriarchy off the hook. Men don't have to do a thing in the lesbian feminist challenge, it's women who have to change and it's women who have to do the work. Thus, lesbian feminism relies on a constant scrutiny of yourself, of your thoughts, of your sexual practice. It is the ultimate 'put your house in order' philosophy. It is this level of scrutiny that has allowed many lesbians to accuse lesbian feminism of being rigid and over-controlling. Lesbian feminism did try to establish certain parameters and certain mores on its new lesbian world – not all of these were workable and not all of these were very consistently applied. Though sex was included in this world view, it was not of primary importance to the movement and was often presented in an idealised way as being much more about women's spiritual communion than a physical experience. Rules against aping heterosexuality or indulging in patriarchal behaviours left some women confused and others quite dissatisfied.

As Lesbian Feminists we may have long discussions with lovers (only) about the guilt, fear and confusion of reproducing modes of behaviour demanded by heterosexuality. Indeed, this is probably one of the major causes of the silence around Lesbian sex: how can we talk openly if we have no way of knowing if our practices are acceptable or not? None of us will speak if we fear being ostracised. Yet we cannot know what is acceptable until we talk.

In private we agonise about the political implications of vaginal or anal penetration, or where 'rough sex' starts and where we decide it is no longer acceptable. Yet politically we rarely discuss sexual practice. If 'sex' is mentioned, it gets converted into an aura mysteriously hanging in the atmosphere – an essence existing between women. It is certainly not something we do.[10]

The idea that lesbian feminists are 'anti-sex' is often used to mean that they are anti-SM. Lesbian feminism sees SM as an abuse of male power, and as such, it simply cannot be compatible with a feminist existence. For lesbian feminists, the rise of SM and its validation within the lesbian community was, and is, both worrying and distressing. It also undermined, and some would say destroyed, the woman-centred universe the lesbian feminists were trying to create. Ultimately it would be the lesbian feminists who were the major casualties in the lesbian sex war. But for them it was a vitally important struggle and they certainly put up a fight.

PART TWO

Lesbian Sex War

Pain Without Gain

Sado-masochism in the spotlight

Lesbian feminism had become the dominating ideology of the early 1980s. But this did not mean that everyone agreed with it. There was a growing perception, both in Britain and the USA, that lesbian feminism had failed to address the nature of lesbian sexuality in any truly meaningful way. The merging of lesbianism into the all-embracing notion of womanhood assumed that you could create a sexuality that was absolutely uniform. It was not enough to talk about sex being about sharing or communing, it was time to talk about sex as sex. This might mean nasty talk about desire and danger, pleasure and pain, fucking and fantasy, but it was only through exploring these issues that lesbians could gain an understanding of the diversity of lesbian sexuality. This was far too much for the lesbian feminists. Francis Williams, editor of the 1990s lesbian magazine *Diva* has described lesbian feminism's approach to sex as a sort of 'sexual veganism'. Suddenly the vegans faced a group of women who wanted to eat red meat. But a quick fuck and raw steak could never be part of the lesbian feminist equation.

It was the rise of a group of self-styled sex radicals that

signalled the beginning of the lesbian sex war. This war was waged on the pages of lesbian newsletters, in books and magazines, in pubs and clubs. Battles were fought in conferences, in cinemas and in the London Lesbian and Gay Centre. On one side were these sex radicals, fighting for what they believed was their right to define their own sexuality and their own sexual practice. On the other side was a lesbian feminist orthodoxy that saw these practices as dangerous and destructive and in total opposition to all that they believed.

In 1981, the American magazine *Heresies* published its 'Sex Issue'. The magazine chose to tackle the issue of lesbian sex and sexuality head on by focusing on some of the most controversial issues – erotica, role-playing, butch and femme and lesbian SM. Amber Hollingbaugh and Cherrie Moraga's article 'What We're Rollin Around in Bed With. Sexual Silences in Feminism: A Conversation Toward Ending Them' best sums up the magazine's approach.

> I think by focusing on roles in lesbian relationships, we can begin to unravel who we really are in bed. When you hide how profoundly roles can shape your sexuality, you can use that as an example of other things that get hidden. There's a lot of different things that shape the way that people respond – some not so easy to see, some more forbidden, as I perceive S/M to be . . . The point is, that when you deny that roles, S/M, fantasy, and/or sexual differences exist in the first place, you can only come up with neutered sexuality, where everybody's got to be basically the same because anything different puts the element of power and deviation in there and threatens the whole picture.[1]

Cherrie Moraga and Amber Hollingbaugh concluded that women should work, go back to consciousness raising groups and build a theory around lesbian sex and sexuality. In this way women could talk about the real issues for lesbians – sex. Oh, if only it could be that simple. Sheila Jeffreys, the lesbian feminist theorist and academic, was clearly deeply angered that one of the great feminist institutions – consciousness raising (CR) – could be used in this way.

> In CR, feminists share experience in order to analyse it and form a critique of male supremacy. We intended to change ourselves and the world, not to worship the status quo. The redefinition made here is profoundly worrying. Of course if a group of lesbians sit together and discuss honestly their sexual feelings, we will hear about SM fantasies, about the ability to get sexual pleasure from fantasies or real humiliation and so on. A CR approach is to ask why this is so – to direct anger at the source of the problem, male supremacy, and to seek to change it and ourselves. The purpose of CR is change and revolution.[2]

Well that settles it then. What Jeffreys' comments signal, is the absolute horror with which many lesbians regarded this new 'dirty talk'. It also shows what would come to be perceived as the intractability of the lesbian position. If CR was about talking about male power, then that is what it would be about. SM sexuality and other male-identified behaviours had no place within its august parameters. Discussion was possible as long as everybody understood from the beginning who was right and who was wrong and who would have to change.

The whole question of desire and women's sexuality caused

a huge row in American feminist circles in 1982. 'Towards a Politics of Sexuality', the Scholar and Feministix Conference held at Barnard College, attempted to 'explore the ambiguous and complex relationship between sexual pleasure and danger in women's lives and in feminist theory'.[3] The Barnard Conference was designed to bring both Feminist and Academic together, but quickly became controversial when radical feminist groups complained that they were not represented on the conference's planning group. American feminism at the time was dominated by the anti-pornography debate and the organising group had not wanted to see this issue overwhelming the conference. The Barnard College authorities began to get immensely jittery when various feminist and anti-porn groups lobbied them. The result of this was that the Conference Diary, a collection of essays reflecting the issues of the conference, was withdrawn and only much later circulated to participants. The Barnard Conference did however focus on issues around women's sexuality that were beginning to become of interest to British feminists and a number of leading British feminists were present.

Though the conference organisers' basic idea was to try and expand notions of what lesbian sexual pleasure might be and to suggest that lesbian sexual contact too had its elements of danger and risk, the conference was widely portrayed as encouraging pornography and pornographic sexual practices like SM and butch/femme role-playing. The Barnard Conference created many rifts in the feminist movement in America. The pornography debate was to continue to be a major issue within American feminism and the role of lesbian-produced porn and erotica was increasingly to form a prominent part in the arguments.

In Britain too, some women were anxious to address the dearth of discussion about desire in lesbian sexuality.

> It seems to us that in the London Women's Liberation Movement (WLM) there is often a chasm between discussions about the 'politics of sexuality' and discussions about what our actual different sexual practices are. Over and over, workshops at conferences, even whole conferences, bill themselves as being about sexuality, only to turn into talk shops about the things which *determine* sexuality, or how frightening it is actually to talk about sex. Evocative words are thrown around, like 'pleasure', 'danger', 'lust', 'romance', but as often as not, on the day, it's other words which apply, like distance, analysis, evasion – and above all, frustration, confusion and boredom.[4]

However, in Britain, debate about desire within lesbian sexuality never really materialised. This was because one issue began to dominate all discussion – SM.

Heresies' 'Sex Issue' also contained a piece by Pat Califia titled, dangerously, 'Feminism and Sadomasochism'. Califia is the *agent provocateur* of the sex radical movement, her writings, and indeed her actions, have long been attacked by lesbian feminists. She has championed the cause of SM and her writings have influenced both her admirers and detractors. In this essay, Califia strives to create a *rapprochement* between feminism and SM as well as providing some key definitions of SM.

> I believe that the society I live in is a patriarchy, with power concentrated in the hands of men . . . Women are

oppressed by being denied access to economic resources, political power, and control over their reproduction . . . An essential part of the oppression of women is the control over sexual ideology, mythology, and behaviour. This social control affects the sexual non-conformist as well as the conformist . . . no individual or group is completely free from erotic tyranny.

Sadomasochism is not a form of sexual assault. It is a consensual activity that involves polarized roles and intense sensations . . . An S/M scene is always preceded by negotiation . . . The bottom is usually given a 'safe word' or 'code action' she can use to stop the scene.

The key word to understanding S/M is fantasy.[5]

Califia is harshly critical of the feminist opponents of SM, accusing them of 'failing to do their homework on human sex-uality' and of being 'like Victorian missionaries in Polynesia . . . interpreting the sexual behaviour of other people according to their own value systems'. Later writings by Califia abandon any idea of *rapprochement*, she becomes as intractably pro-SM as feminists like Sheila Jeffreys are anti.

You might not like the women in my stories . . . They are not completely autonomous human beings, but they chafe under restrictions. You won't get any charity fucks out of them because they don't feel sorry for you. Nor will they say something that will make you feel bad about yourself under the guise of upgrading your id and your politics.[6]

This anger and aggression towards lesbian feminism has become a feature of the pro-SM/anti-SM debate. Califia wants

us to believe that actually it is lesbian feminism that is stop-
ping lesbians leading the lives they want, rather than the
pressures of heterosexual society and oppressive male institutions. In nine years, Califia's patience with lesbian feminism
had clearly largely run out.

In Britain, feminists had discussed SM but mainly in the
context of heterosexual relationships. For them, SM was
another way in which men displayed their sexual power over
women. It was, therefore, deeply shocking to suddenly discover that lesbians were prepared to inflict the same sexual
violence against other lesbians as men were. The arrival of
Heresies' 'Sex Issue' caused some anger among lesbians but
this was little when compared with the fear engendered by the
publication of *Coming to Power*.[7]

Pat Califia was a member of the Samois Collective, an SM
group that published this controversial collection of essays and
stories about lesbian SM. In Britain, *Coming to Power* was
greeted with a mixture of fury and excitement. Sue Golding
reviewed the book in the *London Lesbian Newsletter*, highly
favourably. For Golding, the importance of the book lay not in
its embracing of lesbian SM but in the insights it gave into lesbian sexuality.

> You will have to discover or affirm many general things
> about sex and erotic relationship and fantasies, in
> particular 1. that what we 'do in bed' involves more than
> endless discussion on women's oppression, non-
> monogamy and guilt; 2. that what we 'do in bed' involves
> consensual erotic sexual fantasies/activities that may or
> may not involve the use of leather straps, silk ropes,
> vibrators, orgasms and more than one person; 3. that the

understanding of sex as consensual, erotic, powerful and political constitutes not only the basis of S/M sexual play but the very foundation of Feminism itself.[8]

In autumn 1982, Carolle S. Berry and Carol Jones, writing in the *Revolutionary and Radical Feminist Newsletter* voiced concern at what they perceived to be the growing promotion of SM among lesbians. Interestingly, they agreed that there had been a silence about lesbian sexuality, but they saw this silence as opening the door to a new SM lobby. They issued a warning:

> In writing about sexuality the S/M lobby only write about S/M. This ignores our full sexual potential, whilst narrowing our 'sexuality' down to one small male-created area. S/M is not 'profoundly libertarian', but rather is based on heterosexual rules which are limiting and oppressive – not new at all.[9]

Of course, the notion of narrowing down lesbian sexuality was exactly what the supporters of SM were worrying about. For them the narrowing down of lesbian sexuality into a woman-identified area was equally as unacceptable. Rumours of the horror of some of the stories within the book became somewhat exaggerated. Lesbians and feminists I knew had long and very fearful discussions about what the arrival of the book could mean for lesbians and lesbian sexuality. For the first time, lesbians began to look for SM dykes within their own ranks. Some writers have pointed out that rather than worrying about the distant threat of SM within lesbianism, women would have been wiser focusing on the hidden violence that could lie within lesbian relationships. The demonising of SM could be used to cushion dykes from the difficult realities of lesbian experience.

In 1983 the Lesbian Sex and Sexual Practice Conference in London attempted to break down this silence about lesbian sexuality. Though a range of issues were workshopped, much discussion seemed unfocused and disorganised as there were no speakers to provide a springboard for discussion. Many women still found it very difficult to talk about sex, let alone their deepest desires and fantasies, and they were left with even more questions. There was a highly over-subscribed workshop about SM which some women seemed to have found boringly tame while others found disgustingly up-front. Black lesbian activist Linda Bellos presented a powerful lesbian feminist critique of SM, whilst one young lesbian, Della Disgrace (who reappears in quite another form later in the lesbian sex wars) described how she had fled from the oppressive SM of the Samois lesbians. In actual fact the most contentious part of the conference was that it was held in a building which had no disabled access. For many disabled lesbians, this signified a complete lack of awareness of the needs of disabled lesbians and an assumption that if you had a disability you probably did not have a sexuality.

In 1984, the London Lesbian Strength March was somewhat rocked by the arrival of a small group of very out and very vocal SM dykes marching under a banner of a women's symbol draped in chains. A number of women objected to their presence and they were told that they could not join the march. This came close to causing a scene. After much discussion, it was agreed that they could join the march but only if they promised to stay at the back. This was the first time that sado-masochists had dared to show their faces amongst their lesbian feminist sisters. Women were shocked and angry at their presence and the SM dykes were blamed for ruining the day for the lesbian feminists who felt too appalled and offended to attend. It was the SM dykes who were to blame for their deliberate efforts to destroy what was supposed to be an empowering lesbian occasion. In reality, other lesbians present were actually interested to see the SM dykes there. They certainly did not immediately want them expelled from the massed ranks of dykedom.

However, the most public and bitter row that took place between the pro-SM lobby and lesbian feminists concerned the opening of the London Lesbian and Gay Centre (LLGC).[10] If the Lesbian Strength March had formed an interesting skirmish, and *Coming to Power* had been a shot across the bows, the row about the LLGC really did become the pitched battle of the lesbian sex war. The LLGC had received funding from the GLC which was earmarked for a lesbian-only floor in an otherwise mixed building. Lesbian feminists had not been particularly interested in the LLGC because of its mixed status, until that is, they discovered that SM groups were to be allowed to meet in the building. It was as if this single issue brought all lesbian concern and anger about SM to the surface.

Lesbian feminists formed a group to combat what they saw as the growth of SM and the acceptance of SM as part of the lesbian and gay scene that LLGC's liberal stance clearly demonstrated. Such was the furore caused that an Extraordinary General Meeting was called to discuss the issue. Lesbians Against Sado-Masochism (LASM) packed a mixed Extraordinary General Meeting (EGM) and called for an outright ban on SM groups meeting in the building. However, after a number of procedural difficulties, the meeting was declared unconstitutional and a new EGM was called for a later date.

The arguments around SM and the LLGC were complicated by the increasing growth of identity politics within lesbian feminism. Identity politics creates a hierarchy of oppression and gives space to women from minority groups within the larger grouping to have their say. It had developed as a way of dealing with the inherent racism, classism and ableism of women within a movement that was dominated by white, middle-class women. However, the negative side of this politics was that it could distort argument by placing more weight on who was doing the speaking rather than what they were actually saying. Identity politics could be said to be an early form of political correctness. Like PC, identity politics began as a way of redressing a balance and opening up ideas and discussion, but later it seemed to be a way of pulling rank on your lesbian feminist sisters. The more oppressions you had, the more credence was placed in what you were saying.

In the case of the LLGC, LASM exploited identity politics in two ways.

Lesbian mothers en masse attended one of the general meetings at the new Lesbian and Gay Centre to make their views against sado-masochism known. They made points such as not feeling able to bring their children to a centre in which men and women in black leather and S/M regalia were present since they were struggling hard to rear their children in a way that resisted the sado-society. The lesbian mothers brought their children with them, partly from problems with childcare, but also to make a point. To a background of babies crying some gay men and lesbians sought to hold an abstract intellectual discussion of their right to pursue their pleasures in any way they wished.[11]

By placing lesbian mothers in a sort of moral ascendency, Jeffreys makes any realistic analysis of the EGM impossible. Other women who were present have commented how the over-use of anger and emotion by both sides distorted any sensible argument. While the lesbian mothers' babies were crying, some of those who practised SM were themselves crying at the cruelty of the 'lesbian feminist fascism' that they were facing. And to make matters worse, some of those who supported the SM position were mothers themselves. This was, of course, the other problem with identity politics, because it assumed that all lesbians who shared the same oppressions would share the same opinions.

More importantly, LASM refocused their arguments. They maintained their traditional argument that SM was a manifestation of men's power and violence against women but also added that SM was an inherently fascist (and racist) practice. By using racist scenarios such as mistress punishing slave, or fascist scenarios of Nazi punishing Jew in their sex play, SMers were eroticising power imbalance in ways that many women (both pro- and anti-SM) found quite unacceptable. Lesbian feminists also pointed to SM fashion, much of which seemed to be based on fascist uniforms. Most controversial was the reported sightings of SM dykes wearing swastikas in various lesbian and gay clubs. At the time, as many lesbian feminists seemed to be seeing swastikas as American tourists were seeing the Loch Ness Monster.

Whether SM dykes were regularly brandishing swastikas or not, the concept of 'fascist regalia' was born. But fascist regalia could include anything from whips and chains to the ubiquitous black leather jacket.

> The eroticising of power and oppression in the sexuality of cruelty that is S/M trains us to be turned on by the trappings of fascism. The erotic appeal of fascism, structured into our sexuality as we learn our sexual responses under male supremacy, is enhanced by the politics of S/M. Only the building of an egalitarian sexual practice can fit into anti-fascist politics.
>
> S/M is not a sexual practice which drops from the skies but a response to and echoing of the increasing hold of fascist values and practice in the world outside the gay ghetto.[12]

Jeffreys' paper attempted to show the 'connection between S/M and fascism which we ignore at our peril'. She tried to show how SM (especially among gay men) was an integral part of the growth of Nazism in Berlin in the 1930s. This was something of an over-simplification of German history, based more on a reading of Christopher Isherwood than a full analysis of the causes of the rise of the Third Reich. It was also not very popular with the gay men who were involved in the SM debate. Jeffreys' efforts to create a divide and rule between lesbians and gay men were hampered by the distaste that many lesbians felt at the tactics used.

However, the use of the 'Nazi threat' argument within the LLGC debate and subsequent discussions about the rights and wrongs of SM is interesting. The use of Nazi or racist imagery was not, as lesbian feminists would have everyone believe, an essential part of every SM sex scene. Sheila Jeffreys was quick to spot this and was able to point out that if they weren't actually using these images then SMers were still using others which involved power and humiliation and heterosexism. These might not themselves be racist or fascist but they were part of the same SM/fascist continuum.

> The scenarios of Nazi and Jew or slave and mistress could possibly be left off the agenda by those with tender consciences. This would leave plenty of scope for scenarios and costumes representing sexist oppression . . .
>   Quite apart from the fact that the imagery would remain appallingly sexist and heterosexist, any eroticising of power, any glorifying of oppression can only strengthen the values which maintain all forms of oppression.[13]

Many women were, very rightly, concerned about the use of Nazi, or indeed racist, imagery in SM scenarios but that did not mean that they believed that all SMers were, *ipso facto*, Nazis, racists or fascists. The lesbian feminist argument may have been emotive but its simplistic analysis left women uncomfortable. You simply could not equate the horror of the Third Reich with the wearing of leather jackets or the use of certain scenarios in your sex play.

The sudden lesbian feminist concern with racism came as something of a surprise to a number of black lesbians too. Just as some lesbians had come to feel disenfranchised and depoliticised from the woman-identified woman, black women too felt that their voices had often been silenced. Suddenly lesbian feminists were claiming that they had the most influential voice in fighting racism. 'While it was nice to see lesbian feminism actually addressing racism as a concept, you might have thought they would have asked us what we thought about it first' as one black woman put it to me. The lesbian feminist use of the fear of racism also suggested that lesbian feminists themselves were free of any racism. Black women had long complained that lesbian feminism took a highly tokenistic attitude to race issues and there was often little recognition that the oppression black women faced was any worse than the oppression that white liberal lesbian feminists faced. The lesbian feminist approach also assumed that black women would and should think like them. This was not necessarily the case, there were black lesbians who were either themselves SM dykes or who wanted to debate the issue further. For some black women, lesbian feminism, white dominated as it was, was not the political goal that they wanted to devote their energies to. For some black lesbians, it was important to devote their energies to working with other black lesbians, rather than constantly fighting to have their voices heard within white groupings.

Black women's anger at SM and the use of racist imagery within SM was different to the anger of white lesbian feminists, because they were the ones who had a true understanding, and sometimes experience, of what the promotion of those racist images could mean. At the same time, the issue of racism within the non-SM community was nowhere close to being addressed. Equally, the views and fears of black women could often be ignored by the pro-SM lobby who were much more obsessed with what they saw as the attack on their civil liberties than they were in gaining understanding of another group's oppression.

Gay men were the secondary target in the Nazi/fascist hysteria. Sheila Jeffreys is clear in her understanding that gay men are not the natural allies of the lesbian nation. She saw then, and sees now, the growing linkage between gay men's lives and lesbians' lives as deeply threatening to the lesbian feminist ideal. By placing gay men at the heart of the 'Nazi threat', she was challenging what she saw as the unholy alliance of pro-SM lesbians and gay men at the LLGC.

After the fiasco of the first EGM, the second took place at Conway Hall in London. Acrimony was again the watch-word, but a change of emphasis had taken place. A number of women had become very angered by LASM's tactics at the first meeting. They disliked the fact that the meeting had been 'packed' by a group of women, some of whom were not and never would be Centre users. LASM's easy equation of SM with fascism made women uneasy and their constant use of emotional rather than rational argument did little to advance their cause. Finally, the fact that some of the lesbian feminists seemed to believe that theirs was the only true lesbian view, got right up other women's noses. Better prepared, the anti-LASM wing formed its own group, Lesbians For the Centre, and after a tense vote the LASM group was defeated. LASM had forced a separate lesbian-only vote and, though they did win this, the combined vote overwhelmingly supported the SM groups.

Not all lesbians were as taken with the seriousness of the LLGC debates as others. Activists Liza Power and Linda Semple decided that the only way to deal with the impending horror of the debate was to turn it into a picnic. They caused some wry amusement, as well as a lot of aggravation, when they turned up to the meeting armed with smoked salmon sandwiches and pink champagne. Such was the meeting's tension that when they popped the cork some people really believed there had been gun fire.

There were no real heroes or heroines in the LLGC debates. LASM has been accused of using deeply intimidatory tactics, of shouting women down, of using emotive arguments to impose their will. But one woman who was at the meeting has pointed out that a group of very angry SM dykes, sitting together in SM gear, could be pretty intimidating too. Other women have criticised the very heavy atmosphere at the LLGC and the attitudes of many of the gay men. Activist Julie Bindel sums it up neatly: 'they were not all our gay brothers in nice woolly pullies'. Not every woman was convinced by the SMers' arguments, which tended to be along the lines of 'SM is an expression of our love for women', 'It can't be bad because it's consensual', 'Lesbian feminists are just fascists who want to tell us what we can or can't do in bed.'

Behind many lesbian feminists' anger about SM was a very genuine fear of what SM might represent – they weren't simply 'anti-sex' because they disapproved of their SM sisters. That a challenge had come to lesbian feminist ideology from a group of women who called themselves 'feminist', many of whom had been involved in the WLM, was also deeply distressing. LASM's apocalyptic vision of what the world would be like if SM went unchallenged seems utterly out of proportion, but many of their fundamental certainties were being challenged. The old argument that since SM was patriarchal, lesbian SM must be patriarchal too, was less and less convincing to those lesbians outside the feminist movement. That LASM tried to use Nazi shock tactics was a sign not so much of strength as sheer desperation. SM scared them because they no longer had an answer to it.

Sado-masochism frightens me. It also threatens me.

People who play with it say they are working out power imbalances. I can't understand how you are working something out if you're coming on someone else's pain or coming on your own. Coming beating someone up, or pretending to. That's what I can't get away from. Some get attracted to SM – to the 'thrill' of it, the 'danger' – because it's *formally* forbidden, like porn. But it's all fed into our heads, particularly for women to be masochists. That makes heterosexuality so much easier doesn't it?[14]

But the supporters of SM were fighting for high stakes too. They were fighting against what they saw as lesbian feminism's colonisation of the lesbian identity. Many of those who became dubbed SM apologists did not even have SM sex, but they wanted to be able to talk about it without being told they were Nazis. For those who did enjoy SM sex the fight was partly to be allowed to be what they wanted, with who they wanted, and partly for the right to be a lesbian while doing it. To be branded as a Nazi or as nothing better than a rapist was both distressing and offensive.

Arguments about SM have been made more hazardous by women's failure to find a single acceptable definition of what lesbian SM is. Lesbian feminism created a sort of SM continuum, where any use of sub/dom imagery (doctor and nurse for example), whether in actual sexual practice or in fantasy, was to be seen as morally SM as tying your lover up and cutting her with razor blades. The alternative to this was a sort of sexless wimmin-loving where women come as a result of political penetration – mind-fuck.

Lesbian feminist opposition to SM also emphasised the

way that an acceptance of SM acquiesced with patriarchal power:

> . . . we feel that S/M is a powerful base of male domination. As women our sexuality is targeted and humiliated; stolen and turned against us. Rape and the threat of rape is a means of social control: men seek to make us *want* to be raped. Our oppression is maintained most effectively if we can be made to internalise the pornographic image of women – bound, gagged, silenced, *on our backs*.[15]

But in the same magazine, *Spare Rib*, an interesting critique of this view is contained:

> The issues raised by the S/M debate about sexual power between women require new understandings from us. It's not enough to simply graft an analysis of heterosexual power relationships onto lesbianism. Everything in our lesbian lives, all our experiences, are not simply reducible to interpretation based on reflections or rejections of heterosexuality.[16]

But the SM defence of SM sex is not always totally convincing either. The SM buzzwords, 'Love', 'Trust' and 'Consent' are all very well but an unquestioning acceptance of them can only fit into a fundamentally libertarian politics – a sort of 'anything goes as long we consent to it'.

> I am surprised that the patriarchy has not yet erected a monument to 'Consent', inscribed with the words,

'without which none of this would have been possible'. Perhaps no other concept has confused so many people for so long.

Women 'consent' to: a lifetime of unpaid domestic and sexual service (she wanted to get married); badly paid monotonous work (she took the job); clothing which restricts movement and damages health (no one marched her to the shop at gunpoint); etc., etc.[17]

Pat Califia's assertion that the 'keyword of S/M is fantasy' is interesting. In this view lesbian SM plays out, or re-enacts, certain power differentials and oppressions, it does not replicate them. It can produce a safe arena for acting out the forbidden or the dangerous, it can even be a way for women to take control of their past experiences. Cherry Smyth remembers one Jewish woman talking very powerfully and passionately of her right to use Nazi imagery in her lovemaking as a way of taking control of the fact that she had lost most of her family in the concentration camps. 'To me that seemed strategic and practical, I could understand her using it. But it was a shock to me to think that feminism had failed to cleanse her horror.'

I have heard some lesbians make great claims for SM as a cathartic experience. Indeed, other women have used SM to come to terms with their own experiences of rape, sexual violence and abuse. This is, I believe, something that only an individual lesbian can claim from her own individual experience. I am as nervous when SM is portrayed as our universal panacea as I am when lesbian feminism is.

SM depends on playing on the power imbalance between two lovers, the active and passive, the top or bottom. The fact

that the two (or more) participants are lesbians, means that the
dynamic is different than that between a heterosexual man
and a woman. Thus, it is possible for a lesbian SM scene to be
based on equality rather than inequality. This is very hard for
those opposed to SM to stomach. As Julie Bindel put it:

> SM plays out inequality. If you look how inequality is
> played out between black and white, men and women, SM
> takes that, plays on it and then eroticises it. Our sexuality
> does effect who we are as people. If a man is sexually
> violent then it does define him as a person, it defines his
> perception of sex and the class of women. Sex is never in a
> vacuum. There is no such thing as 'this is just what we do
> in the bedroom'.

There is no doubt that some negative responses to SM are
motivated as much by the 'yuk' factor as the usual political
sensibilities.

> First we have the safety chapter. The fact that there's a
> need for advice on how not to hospitalise/kill each other
> during an SM scenario is pretty dodgy, but wait until you
> read it![18]

It is, of course, rather difficult to create a meaningful political ideology around the right to give your lover an enema. 'I
face enough oppression in my life for simply being a lesbian,
without wanting to go home and have my partner piss on me'
as one lesbian I spoke to put it.

Neither were lesbian feminists particularly convinced by
the concept of 'safety' within a lesbian SM context. Simply,

they did not believe that the 'safe words' would work. This concern was reinforced in 1982 when Pat Califia faced prosecution in the States for carving a swastika, allegedly without consent, on her lover's arm.

Although most of the arguments about SM were couched in political terms, the concerns that many lesbians had about the safety of SM sex reveal that there was a strongly personal element in their opposition to it. Whilst it was theoretically possible to bury the personal within the political, arguments around SM were so bitter and antagonistic precisely because women on both sides of the debate found it hard to discuss SM in anything but very personal terms. Sex can have political overtones, it can be a political choice but it remains an intensely personal experience. Thus, it is rather different criticising someone for what they do in bed than for their position on a single European currency.

The growth of identity politics within the movement meant that this personalisation continued. When lesbian feminists began to draw political parallels between SM and fascism, the result was to name those who supported or practised SM sex as fascists. The horrible irony was that the more extreme the anti-sex lobby became, the more justified the pro-SM lobby felt. They felt that their right to have lesbian sex as they wanted was being challenged in the most despicable and hysterical way. Their response was to turn the argument against lesbian feminists, accusing them of trying to police lesbianism and lesbian sexuality. Thus lesbians could be fascist for not being SM and lesbians could be fascist for having SM sex. The rights and wrongs of SM itself became impossible to debate in an atmosphere of fascist name-calling.

There was also a sort of protectionism that was circulating

among some of those opposed to SM at the time. They felt that lesbians could be seduced into an SM life-style and this might be particularly dangerous for younger lesbians coming out on the scene. The 'protect our little children' argument rings alarm bells in many a lesbian's or gay man's ears, as it is usually used as an excuse to stop us being parents or sack us from our jobs. It is also patronising and inconsistent. To suggest that lesbians could be the victims of female power as wielded by the dastardly SM dykes was not only to reassign women their old victim status but to totally under-estimate the real power that patriarchy wields in the wider society. The reality was, of course, that as much as lesbian feminists could cry wolf about the Nazi threat, as much as they would try to put their own house in order, the enemy of lesbianism was heterosexuality. With or without the SM dykes, lesbians were still as far away from the lesbian feminist utopia as ever.

Nor have SMers ever really come up with a convincing response to the many lesbians, black or white, who were frightened by the inherent racism that much SM fashion, and indeed fantasy, presented. We have seen one example of how, for one woman, SM was a practical way of facing her own history and experience, but it is hard to see how two white lesbians enacting a slave/master scenario could do the same. When lesbians were playing around with racist imagery and the power imbalances that racism creates, it was not their own history of oppression that they were playing with. There is a clear difference between the oppression of white lesbians and the oppression of black lesbians; debates around SM tend to illustrate this basic reality. As the 1980s progressed, the issue of racism within radical sexuality was swept under the carpet. The existence of black lesbians who themselves practice SM has been used to suggest that concerns about racism within sexual play were unnecessary.

The events at the London Lesbian and Gay Centre did cause as many rifts within lesbianism and feminism as the Barnard Conference had done in America. Though the argument at the LLGC had been about SM, the lesbian feminist position has more often been portrayed as 'anti-sex' as the pro-SM lobby began to re-colonise lesbian sex. These battles are firmly placed within the politics of the London lesbian community. For many lesbians living beyond the M25, these debates were somewhat irrelevant. Lesbians across the country did not automatically don SM gear, nor did lesbian feminists pack their bags and move to Lesbos. A number of women did come out in various local lesbian communities as SM dykes but they were greatly in the minority. Many lesbians throughout the country shared the lesbian feminist concern about SM while being bewildered at the ferocity of the row in London. Lesbian feminism's position as the dominating political ideology was essentially safe at the end of the row at the LLGC, but a new pro-sex coalition was building. These women did want to talk about SM, they did want to talk about their sexual practice, they did want to read books, see films and look at lesbian erotica. It was here that the seeds of the late 1980s lesbian sexual permissiveness were sown. And it was here that the lesbian sex wars would finally be won or lost.

Breaking Down the Barriers

The 'Lesbian Summer of Love'

The row about SM in London in the mid-1980s marked the beginning of a change in how lesbians regarded both their sexuality and their sexual practice. For some, the mere existence of SM within the lesbian scene illustrated a frightening return to patriarchal values, the values that condoned racism, sexism and violence against women. Others saw the right of women to express an SM sexuality as being little different from the fundamental right of all women to express their sexuality in whatever way they choose.

Nevertheless, the arguments around SM opened up a channel of discussion about lesbian sexuality that hitherto had only been possible within the narrow confines of social, rather than political, groupings. It was one thing to talk positively about SM with a group of mates in the pub on a Saturday night and quite another to bring the subject up at a lesbian discussion group. As the 1980s progressed, it almost seemed as if women were getting used to the idea of SM, and a certain tolerance of the possibility of SM, and indeed a desire for information about SM, became more widespread. What was needed was a new openness about SM, and indeed non-SM, lesbian sexuality. In the summer of 1988 a number of events, discussions and a controversial film tried to make this lesbian *perestroika* occur.

In July 1988, the Lesbian Archive organised a lesbian summer school. Women came from all over Britain to enjoy workshops and discussions on various aspects of lesbian politics. However, the summer school was overwhelmed by a major argument over the showing of Sheila McLaughlin's lesbian film *She Must be Seeing Things*.[1] McLaughlin's film was vastly different from the usual lesbian cinematic fare. It was not a soapy romance *à la Desert Hearts*[2] nor a heterosexual version of a lesbian affair *à la Lianna*.[3] And most importantly, the film did not idealise lesbian relationships. In the Queer 1990s we are confident enough in our own sexuality not to need the compulsory happy ending that seemed to dominate what little cinema, theatre and literature there was around for lesbians in the 1970s and 1980s. We are also less afraid of art that asks us more difficult questions about ourselves and our sexuality. *She Must be Seeing Things* was one of the first films to stretch our boundaries about what could be acceptable as lesbian cinema. It was therefore inevitable that it would cause controversy.

The film focuses on the relationship of two lovers, Agatha and Jo. Agatha becomes obsessed with the idea that her lover is having an affair with a man. As a result of this, for no apparent reason, she dresses up as a man and goes to a sex shop to buy a dildo; she also has a number of violent fantasies about her lover's death and/or mutilation. Along the way, there is a sex scene between Agatha and Jo where the 'femme' Jo, wearing the archetypal frilly underwear, is tied up by her 'butch' partner. This was hot stuff. And though much of the anger about the film was to focus on the SM sex, the possibility of violence between women and the playing-out of a butch/femme scenario (which for some women was the same as the SM one), it was also very clear that many women were made intensely uncomfortable and angry at seeing a 'warts and all' portrayal of a lesbian relationship. Lesbian films were supposed to be affirming, they were not supposed to be discomforting and challenging.

Even before *She Must be Seeing Things* was released in Britain it became dubbed an SM movie. Some women, therefore, at the previewing of parts of the film at a summer school event about lesbians in film, stormed the stage, while others tried to rip the film out of the video machine. Cherry Smyth and Inge Blackman, the women who were showing the film and who chaired the discussion afterwards, were later to be accused of deliberately engineering an 'SM dynamic which left many lesbians distraught and crying'.[4]

Other showings of the film were also marked by protests. In Manchester an attempt was made to stop the film showing by placing a fake bomb in the ladies' lavatory. At some showings women created 'safe spaces' where women, no doubt overwhelmed by the appalling horror of it all, could have their feminist consiousnesses cleansed.

But did *She Must be Seeing Things* really deserve all the anger and controversy it created? And was it an SM film as such, or were the scenes within it explicitly SM? What was clear was that not all women, whether at the summer school or at other showings in the country, were really ready to answer these questions. At the picket at the Manchester showing, many of the women had not seen the film themselves but had been told it was explicitly SM and that was enough. It is interesting to see that much of the discussion about the film was focused more strongly on whether it should be shown at all rather than on the film's actual merits. For some women this has been interpreted as a clear example of how the lesbian feminist line (opposing the film vehemently) could be used not to engender discussion but to prevent and close off discussion of 'sensitive' lesbian issues altogether. Certainly bomb hoaxes and stage-storming were extreme reactions. In Bradford, a group of lesbians opposed to the film managed to prevent one of its screenings by pouring cement down the cinema's toilets. This was highly unpopular with many of the not inconsequential numbers of lesbians in Bradford. The cinema had always made an effort to be supportive of lesbian and gay events and there was some fear that they might be reluctant to support lesbian cinema in the future. Most importantly, the group's actions were considered to be highly undemocratic. Lesbians wanted to decide about the film for themselves. This kind of high-minded behaviour won the film's opponents few friends.

But what was there in the film that suggested to lesbians that they should indulge in the equivalent of book-burning to protect other lesbians from its terrible message? That two lesbians should be portrayed as using bondage (i.e. SM) in their sex play was deeply shocking; that a woman would not only wear men's clothes but then go out to buy a dildo was even worse. In fact, the film was trying to *subvert* the stereotypical image of lesbians as 'just women trying to be men', not emphasise it. For McLaughlin, the character is using her male disguise to challenge and defeat maleness – she does not want to be a man.[5] Criticism of the film also focused on Agatha's violence towards her partner, though it often neglected to point out that the violence is only ever part of Agatha's fantasy – it never actually takes place. As for the SM scene, the first time I saw the film I dropped off to sleep at the crucial moment and missed it; the second time I remained wide awake but spent the whole film waiting to see when the controversial SM scene was going to happen.

It would be wrong to suggest that the women who saw the film and actively opposed it were not genuinely angered by it. The question is whether they were angered by what they saw or by what they thought they saw – not so much a case of 'she must be seeing things' but a whole feminist dynamic. For one woman the film represented a 'curiously male view, that our relationships were somehow about power and domination. I thought the film was blatantly dishonest.' A showing of the film at an event in Edinburgh a couple of years later created a rather different view. Women were disappointed in its artistic merits and slightly surprised that it had engendered so much conflict.

The portrayal of a lesbian relationship in crisis does make the viewer uncomfortable, and the film does raise difficult issues about possessiveness and jealousy in lesbian relationships. What is highly questionable about the film is the use of race: Agatha, the 'butch' with all her fantasy violence and jealousy, is black, whilst Jo the innocent 'femme', is white. In many ways *She Must be Seeing Things* was simply ahead of its time – women weren't used to seeing images of themselves that were both negative and challenging. That the film called itself a 'lesbian' film was difficult for those women who refused to see that there could be anything possibly lesbian in the scenes that it depicted. Whether the violence existed in reality or in fantasy made no difference, this was nothing more than an echo of the old SM defence that SM was merely a playing out of the fantasies that deep down all lesbians enjoy.

Summer 1988 was also to see the publication of Joan Nestle's collection of essays and short stories, *A Restricted Country*.[6] Nestle herself is both one of the founders of New York's Lesbian Herstory Archives and a committed champion of butch/femme history. Her work marries together a historical perspective of butch/femme and a passionate belief in its validity as an expression of lesbian sexuality. This is important as butch/femme has often been portrayed not as a manifestation of a specifically lesbian sexuality but merely as a sexual practice that mimics, and therefore validates, heterosexuality. Nestle believes that just as lesbians share a history of experience we also share an erotic history too. This 'erotic heritage', as she calls it, has shaped how we regard ourselves and our sexuality; it should not therefore be expunged from our history books because it does not suit current political ideologies.

Nestle's work is appealing because she brings both the intensely personal and the political to her work. Her experiences as a femme lesbian in the American bar scene of the 1950s is central to her political message. Rather than disowning her butch past as other writers have done, she embraces it and tries to show us that, regardless of the strictures of the time, butch/femme was in fact a powerful declaration of lesbian sexuality – in itself an act of defiance and courage and also in its own sphere, political. For Nestle it is our modern interpretation of lesbian history that has left butch/femme so stigmatised.

I believe, however, that many pre-Stonewall Lesbians were feminists, but the primary way this feminism – this autonomy of sexual and social identities – was expressed, was precisely the form of sexual adventuring that now appears so oppressive.[7]

But Joan Nestle has also been open to attack for being hostile towards lesbian feminism. Nestle clearly feels that much lesbian feminist writing not only devalues the experiences of the butch/femme lesbians of the 1950s and 1960s, but also rewrites them and recreates them as non-lesbian. She disputes what she sees as the tendency of some lesbian feminists to believe that acceptable lesbianism only became possible with the arrival of lesbian feminism. Most importantly she is clear in her criticism of political lesbianism.

> We lesbians from the fifties made a mistake in the early seventies: we allowed our lives to be trivialised and reinterpreted by feminists who did not share our culture. The slogan 'Lesbianism is the practice and feminism is the theory' was a good rallying cry, but it cheated our history.[8]

This comment echoes the criticisms of some British feminists (see Wendy Clark) to what they saw as the over-emphasis of lesbianism as a political choice rather than a genuine sexual identity of its own. By drawing on butch/femme history and giving it back its place in lesbian history, Nestle is laying down a clear challenge to lesbian feminism.

However, much of the power of *A Restricted Country* lies in the sheer passion with which Nestle defends her lesbian history. Nestle is clear in her recognition of the importance of feminism for lesbianism, she just does not accept that her experiences and those of many other lesbians contemporary to her should be forgotten. She wants her readers to understand 'the complexity and diversity of resistance, the nonchalance of courage, and the tenacity of those who are different'.[9] For her, lesbians are framed as much by the erotic heritage that the butches and femmes of the 1950s and 1960s represent as they are by the political advances made by lesbian feminists in the 1970s and 1980s. There is, thus, a clear relationship between Nestle the archivist and Nestle the political polemicist. For her, history and sexuality are gloriously bound up with each other. It is an interesting irony that Sheila Jeffreys, so often opposed to Nestle's message, should have been a co-founder of Britain's lesbian archive. Whilst Britain's archive remains a much valued and highly significant resource, it is somewhat devalued by its failure to include certain key texts which are considered unacceptable in a lesbian feminist context. A scan of the archive shelves would suggest that no British lesbian had ever been introduced to the grisly possibilities of SM sex.

In A Restricted Country Nestle is also highly concerned about what she sees as the growing moves towards censorship within lesbian feminist circles. In America, feminists and lesbians had been involved in many, highly destructive arguments about pornography. Between 1985 and 1986, leading feminists Andrea Dworkin and Catherine MacKinnon had formed a strange alliance with the highly right-wing Meese Commission on Pornography in their opposition to all forms of pornography. Many feminists felt that the feminist anti-pornography movement had been hijacked by Meese and that the Commission was merely using the right-on language of feminism to enforce a rigid right-wing agenda. It was felt then that the Commission talked about obscene imagery; its first targets were those images that presented lesbian and gay life-styles or sexuality. At the same time, lesbians and feminists themselves were involved in often complex arguments about whether portrayals of butch/femme or SM sexual scenarios were pornographic or merely erotic. Many lesbians had begun to feel that sexual imagery produced by lesbians and for lesbians should have no place in lesbian magazines or literature, let alone the lesbian consciousness. Nestle herself began to find that some of her work was being censored or was being criticised for being pornographic and therefore anti-lesbian. For Nestle, the feminist and lesbian attack on so-called pornography mirrored what she had seen of the McCarthy witch hunts of the 1950s. It is this double attack of the right-wing on the outside and a prescriptive feminism on the inside that Nestle felt was so dangerous. By trying to create a perfect, unsullied notion of lesbianism, many anti-pornography lesbians were leaving their transgressive sisters at the mercy of an extreme right-wing philosophy.

In Nestle's work, both butch/femme and SM are part of our erotic lesbian heritage. They cannot be removed from our collective consciousness because, whether we like it or not, they are part of our sexual experiences and erotic heritage. Many of the short stories within *A Restricted Country* portray a highly physical lesbian sexuality. Nestle is not afraid to talk about the exchange of power within butch/femme sexuality – she is not afraid to write about fist-fucking or sex toys. Even in this area, her work is characterised by the intense sense of her own personality that she brings to the work, both fiction and non-fiction. When Nestle writes about sex, highly physical sex, sex that some women might easily describe as SM, she does not write in the distancing, often rather detached way that other sex writers do. She is not a Pat Califia, who often uses an aggressive and confrontational style in writing her SM scenarios. Rather, by placing herself and her history side by side with her own fiction, she actually makes the sex seem integral to the personalities and people involved, rather than strangely other. Nestle never denies that power is at the heart of butch/femme sexual practice, but for her this use of power, or display of power, is not abusive – it is more about finding one's own sense of power in a hostile environment. Thus, Nestle herself is making the clear connection between butch/femme and what lesbian feminism would describe as an SM sexual dynamic. Nestle's notion of an erotic heritage that played with lesbian sexual power to challenge heterosexual power is appealing. It suggests that lesbianism can have both a political and a sexual power. It is very different from the lesbian feminist approach that seems to suggest that the sexual can be utterly subsumed by the political.

Lesbian feminist writers like Julia Penelope in the States (who experienced butch/femme for herself) and Sheila Jeffreys in Britain have been quick to challenge Nestle for what they see as both an idealisation and a romanticising of butch/femme relationships. Both writers have attempted to show how women were devalued by the experience of butch/femme role-playing and how oppressive that life-style was. They point out that sex roles were often rigidly defined and that the femme was often treated as little more than a domestic drudge. They see the butches and femmes as a part not so much of a glorious lesbian heritage but of a victimised lesbian past. They also refute what they see as Nestle's assertion that it was feminism that effectively silenced butch/femme history and experience. We have already seen how in Britain in the

1960s it was lesbians themselves, through the magazine *Arena 3* and through meetings and discussion, who began to question the need for butch/femme relationships within the lesbian 'scene'.

> The implication of Nestle's writing is that somehow feminists imposed egalitarian forms of relationship upon lesbians in the late '60s and early '70s. This suggests that the feminist prescription came from outside the lesbian community, from political theorists who knew nothing about role-paying from the inside.[10]

The very fact that Nestle's view of butch/femme is based so firmly in her own personal experience leads to its own difficulties. It lays Nestle open to attack for idealisation of a scene that could be oppressive and which reflected the oppression of straight society. The violence and harassment that many butch lesbians faced from heterosexual society was often reflected in violence between lesbians in the clubs and violence within individual relationships. Audre Lord, in her autobiographical book *Zami: A New Spelling of my Name* points to the inherent racism of the butch/femme scene:

> The Black women I usually saw . . . were tough in a way I felt I could never be. Even if they were not, their self-protective instincts warned them to appear that way. By white america's racist distortions of beauty, Black women playing 'femme' had very little chance in the Bag [the Bagatelle, a lesbian bar.[11]

In Nestle's desire to reclaim her piece of lesbian history,

she can seem over-indignant with lesbian feminist writers. And just as she criticises some lesbian feminists for neglecting butch/femme and taking it out of its historical context, so also some 1980s and 1990s lesbians have idealised the notion of butch/femme courage and taken it out of its context too.

Some women did characterise some of the stories in *A Restricted Country* as distinctly SM. Butch/femme, with its notion of role-playing and exchange of power, certainly encapsulates the old SM notion of 'power and trust'. But it is interesting to note that the publication of *A Restricted Country* in Britain was not as controversial as might have been expected. The charm and personality of Nestle herself came across strongly in the readings she gave and discussions she led about the book. Those women who criticised the SM or the celebration of role-playing they saw in the book were not answered defensively, but rather with great honesty. Some women did walk out of Nestle's readings, others simply did not attend. Readings also attracted a large lesbian leather crowd. But there certainly were not the bomb hoaxes, the pickets, or the stand-up rows that had greeted *She Must be Seeing Things*. For some, this is proof of a sort of SM fatigue that had hit lesbian feminist circles; others believe that women were simply genuinely interested in what Nestle was saying. For others still, McLaughlin's film had been dangerous because it was distributed nationally as a lesbian film and they saw cinema as having a far wider audience than a lesbian book published by an independent feminist publishing house. And yet others have argued that lesbian feminists had far more important things to worry about than one lesbian's take on lesbian herstory.

The publishing of *A Restricted Country* rekindled the

debate about butch/femme and role-playing within the lesbian community in Britain, but in a slightly different way than it did in the States. In America, the thirteen-year research project of Elizabeth Kennedy and Madeline Davis into the butch/femme scene in Buffalo, New York[12] again focused on the courage of the butch/femme pioneers, though it did not shy away from showing some of the grimmer realities of the scene. In Britain, we lack any similar research into butch/femme life-styles, and this has led to a certain ignorance about this part of our own history. At the same time, I believe that for many years butch/femme has been shrouded in a sort of feminist 'cringe factor'. However, reclamation of butch/femme so inimical to a lesbian feminist world view, became inevitable as sex radicalism grew among lesbians in the late 1980s.

The embracing of butch/femme among British lesbians in the late 1980s was rather different from that of the 1950s. Butch/femme had become much more about sexual practice than an integration of lesbian history and sexual experience. Nestle herself dislikes the notion of butch/femme as simple 'role-playing'; for her it is something much more – an integral part of her own sexuality. For us, butch/femme or role-playing has become inextricably linked to SM sexual behaviour. This is because butch/femme is now visualised as being much more about the exchange of power within an individual sex scene than as a form of lesbian survival or an individual identity. In the 1995 lesbian sex guide *Making Out: The Book of Lesbian Sex and Sexuality*,[13] notions of butch or femme have been totally replaced by the concept of 'submission and dominance'. Less contentious than unhelpful labels, perhaps, but also more an aping of our erotic heritage than an embracing of it.

In a purely sexual context, role-playing is about playing

with notions of power. Nobody lies there and does it and says
'I'm doing this for Joan Nestle.' Like SM, which some women
would say it is anyway, role-playing has become a symbol of
how lesbians can transgress from other lesbians. To a certain
extent the research of Kennedy and Davis, or the writings of
Nestle and others, become highly convenient. They give lesbians a path to transgression. It is interesting to see how the
publicity and credibility given to role-playing and SM has
increased at the same rate that the lesbian feminist voice has
become silenced. The re-arrival of a role-playing dynamic
coincides with the arrival of a newer generation powered by
anger at the Thatcher decade and the iniquity of Section 28.
For some, the need to empower oneself in the bedroom feeds
into the need to empower oneself in the workplace or on the
street. The increased sex radicalism of the late 1980s is an
interesting reflection of what was actually a rather poor time
politically for lesbians and gay men.

So did that mean that lesbian feminists were right all
along? Was role-playing just a socially constructed response to
the oppression of homophobic society? A way of coping with
oppression not actually dealing with it? If Section 28 represented a retrograde step for lesbian and gay politics, it also
fuelled a new energy and commitment amongst lesbians and
gay men. The end of the 1980s saw an increased radicalism
with the arrival of the political lobbying group Stonewall and
the more radical direct action group Outrage. Clearly, the
context had changed. Heterosexual society could still be
oppressive but the lesbians of the late 1980s did not just have
to survive – they also had the confidence to fight back. This
was a very different scene from the butch/femme scene of the
1950s and 1960s. If lesbians had the confidence to challenge

heterosexual society they also had the confidence to keep pushing at the boundaries of lesbian sexual mores.

Nevertheless, butch/femme identity remains a problematic area for many lesbians. Is there such a thing today as an inherently butch lesbian? Or is 'butchness' just a social construct, a set of behaviours brought upon us by the pressures we face from a heterosexual society? Lesbian feminism is founded on the notion that lesbianism is socially constructed – there can be no such thing as the biologically determined, essential lesbian. But notions of butchness or femmeness still create many problems for us. We are actually no nearer understanding what butch and femme really mean for us, if anything at all, than we were twenty-five years ago. There are lesbians who believe that they are biologically born butch or born femme, there are lesbians who believe that somehow we all have a psychological essence of butch/femme memory lodged within us. For others, butch/femme remains proof of the duality of masculinity and femininity that runs through every woman. Amidst all this theory, we are probably better off limiting our understanding of butch/femme to something we do in the bedroom, something we do with our wardrobes and our haircuts and, of course, our histories. than to try to delve deep into our lesbian psyches.

Nestle's promotional tour with *A Restricted Country* ended with a full-scale panel discussion called 'Putting the Sex back into Sexual Politics'. It is said that nearly three hundred lesbians, and even some gay men, attended the debate. The meeting focused on pornography and censorship and the panel represented a good spectrum of views, including two women from the more radical lesbian feminist camp. But the discussion was felt by many to be rather unsuccessful. Peaceful it may have been, but nobody was very sure about what it had actually achieved, whether the sex could be put back into sexual politics, or if it had ever been taken out in the first place.

The summer of 1988 also saw the last Lesbian Strength March. This was marred by a row between SM dykes and other dykes on the march, in a similar way to when Strength had been derailed by a protest in 1984. Those supporting SM turned up in a much larger contingent and their banner was somewhat provocative. All the confidence that had been created by the recent activism around Section 28 was lost in the general row about the presence of SM dykes. As a result of this débâcle, a public panel discussion about lesbian SM was planned.

The Face to Face video production company tried to organise a discussion of the role of SM in lesbian sexuality. Although nearly two hundred women turned up for the discussion, the event was somewhat hampered when Sheila Jeffreys, the 'anti-SM campaigner' (as the *Pink Paper* put it) failed to turn up. She felt that the panel for the discussion was grievously imbalanced, even though she was not the only speaker opposing SM (campaigner and Labour counsellor Linda Bellos was the other). The result of her decision was, of course, to unbalance the discussion. What could have been an interesting and passionate argument became virtually a free advertisement for the joys of SM and the lesbian SM nightclub Chain Reaction. The positive result of this was a certain demystification of SM. However, some women were rather critical of what they saw as an opportunity squandered as the afternoon turned into a sort of SM revivalist meeting. The *Pink Paper* was rather more optimistic. It felt that 'There was a mood of optomism [sic] that after years of wrangling a precedent for productive discussion had been set.'[14] The small handful of black lesbians who attended the discussion were disappointed. They felt that their questions about the inherent racism of SM were ignored and their concerns discounted. When the *Pink Paper* wrote about productive discussion they felt this was more about saying good things about SM than really looking at the issue in any detail.

Amidst the events of the so-called 'Lesbian Summer of Love', it is interesting to note that throughout this time London had actually played host to its very own lesbian SM club. First opened in 1987, Chain Reaction had become highly successful. It even survived an infamous assault from a group of very angry anti-SM dykes. A group of women from Lesbians Against Sado-Masochism (so it is said) attacked the club with crowbars and threatened some of the women there. That a group of women who criticised SM as being violence against women should themselves take up 'arms' and threaten other lesbians was seen as both hysterical and unreasonable. No doubt the threat to the poor SM girls that night was greatly exaggerated, but nevertheless a picture was created of the anti-SM dykes as being just as scary as their SM sisters.

1989 saw a series of workshops in London which attempted to break down some of the taboos around lesbian sexuality. This was a serious attempt to ask questions about lesbian sexuality and was felt to be particularly relevant in an age when HIV and AIDS were becoming issues of increasing importance for lesbians. At the same time, in the North of England, some lesbians were beginning to try and explore the issue of lesbian sexuality further. *Scene Out*, the North-west's lesbian magazine, brought out its 'Sex Issue', which attempted to talk about SM, power in lesbian relationships and the nature of lesbian relationships themselves. But not all women were ready, or indeed interested, in this new lesbian sexual openness. At the same time as a new commercialism around sexuality was growing in London, with the arrival of the sex magazine *Quim* and the mail order sex toy catalogue *Thrilling Bits* there was also a groundswell of women who were unmoved by all this exciting talk of naughty new lesbian sexuality.

In Manchester, in the summer of 1990, a one-off club night called The Lesbian Summer of Love at the city's ferociously trendy Hacienda, caused a stir. That the club set out to attract the more dangerously sexual lesbian was bound to create controversy. The event itself was little more than the usual lesbian disco. However, there were women in leather at the event and some of them did indeed take their tops off and dance bare-breasted on the stage. Historically, lesbians have quite a history of taking their tops off and dancing at lesbian discos – this phenomenon could be seen just as often at right-on women's discos in the early 1980s as it could in sex clubs in the late 1980s and early 1990s. What was different was that a lesbian club in Manchester had actually welcomed SM dykes in, and it was they who had taken off their waistcoats. The event became slightly farcical when one of its organisers, no doubt moved by the emotion of the occasion, gave a deeply passionate and largely incoherent speech in defence of the evening. This was interpreted by some of the anti-SM dykes there as a sort of SMers' Charter. As a result, a meeting was called some days after the event by a group of women deeply concerned by what they saw as the worrying rise of SM in lesbian venues in Manchester.

For the women who organised this meeting SM seemed to

be the root cause of racism, fascism and violence within the scene. The general tone of the meeting seemed to be that if you removed the SM dykes from Manchester, violence, aggression and racism would magically go with them. This seemed a highly simplistic analysis, but the organisers' defence of the club – basically that they just wanted to celebrate lesbian luv and the diversity of lesbian sexuality – seemed pretty simplistic too. What was all too clear was that the two groups were coming from vastly different world views and that these were unlikely ever to be reconciled.

A lesbian workshop at the 1990 International Lesbian and Gay Association Conference in Stockholm focused, amongst many other issues, on generational conflicts within lesbian politics. There is a clear conflict between generations of lesbians when it comes to issues like SM and butch/femme. When a more sex radical generation of lesbians rail against their lesbian feminist sisters for being sex fascists there is clearly an element of teenage rebellion involved here. As lesbians have grown confident in their own sexuality, so they have also been able to play around with notions of that same sexuality. What was once forbidden becomes excitingly dangerous and enticing.

In the 1980s there was a newer generation of lesbians, often accompanied by lesbians who had been around for a while, who wanted to bring their new ideas and energies to their lesbian world. They also, unconsciously and consciously, reflected the different worlds from which they were coming. The decade of the 1980s brought a tremendous change to lesbian and feminist politics. The collective ideas of the 1970s were gradually dispelled as the 1980s progressed and economic realities took their place. As more emphasis was placed on individualism the pleasure of the individual became more important than that of the body politic. This difference in perspective was bound to create its own tensions. Many lesbians have not, in fact, been shaken from their belief in the rightness of the lesbian feminist analysis. However, these views have been overtaken, and therefore often silenced, by a new generation who reflect the values of the more commercialised, commodified 1990s. I believe lesbian feminism's greatest weakness has been its failure to even think about ways it might adapt to the needs of a differing world. Lesbian feminism's anger, and even occasional fits of violence against the forms of sexual behaviour it dislikes, suggests that it never really understood how seriously many dykes needed and wanted to discuss the limits of their own sexuality. By creating the taboo, they actually made the exploration of that taboo inevitable and, indeed, exciting. Much of the argument between sex radical or SM dykes and their lesbian feminist sisters have been created by the need for each generation to persuade the other that they are the ones who are right.

A letter in *Feminist Review* in spring 1990, responding to an earlier article chronicling events during the summer of 1988, roundly criticises the whole concept of a summer of lesbian sex.[15] The writers point out that a group of two hundred or so London lesbians charging about talking about SM, role-playing and lesbian sexuality hardly heralded anything very important. But in many ways that lesbian summer in 1988 did mark a change in lesbian attitudes to lesbian sexuality.

It was a coincidence that *She Must be Seeing Things* and *A Restricted Country* should appear within such a short time of each other, but they both opened doors to new ideas and new thoughts about sexuality. Joan Nestle's book, for example, is a passionate defence of a time that has been greatly derided. But is the notion of 'erotic heritage' anything more than a clever con to justify a power-abusing sexual practice? Nestle's book at least allows lesbians a whole new take on these sexual practices and ideas and the reclamation of the history of butch/femme gave the whole concept of role-playing a new veneer of respectability. At the same time, the summer of 1988 suggested that if there was not yet wholesale acceptance then there was a certain toleration towards a more radical practice of lesbian sex. Arguments that had seemed so vitally important to lesbian well-being in 1985 just did not have the same significance in 1988. The very success of the lesbian feminist movement in bringing dykes out and proud into the 1980s, also made the creation of new ideas and new opinions inevitable.

By the end of the 1980s, the lesbian sex wars were over. The intransigence of the lesbian feminist position, with its occasional use of dubious tactics and hysterical argument, was at odds with a new sexual radicalism that seemed daring and exciting. Lesbian sexual practice would continue to be an important issue for many lesbians as the 1990s brought new changes to the lesbian scene. But the angry and the passionate debates about lesbian sexuality were largely over. Lesbian feminism retains many dedicated adherents, it has not conveniently gone away while we all go out and buy our dildos, but its power as a political ideology that could embrace a lesbian nation has been lost. And that power was lost partly because the world changed around lesbian feminism and partly because we could not agree about a little thing like our own sexual practice. The same movement that challenged the weaponry of mass destruction at Greenham Common became lost in so much cement down a cinema toilet.

Getting Wet

Lesbians talk dirty

It's not surprising that after all the shenanigans of the 'Lesbian Summer of Love', lesbians would want to put their feet up and read a few dirty books. In less than a decade lesbians had moved from being rigidly silent about lesbian sex to being vociferously, if not voraciously, sexual. The publication of both *Serious Pleasure* and *Quim* magazine brought writing about lesbian sex into the spotlight. *Thrilling Bits*, the first British mail order sex toy company pulled dildos out of the closet and put them back in the bedroom. A new commercialism was growing around lesbian sex and sexuality and a new generation of lesbians began to espouse sex rather than sexual politics.

These days we rather take mail order sex toys for granted: you can try Shhh, Belt up and Buckle Off, Aphrodite, etc. The 1988 *Thrilling Bits* catalogue suggested that perhaps its owners didn't take the whole sex business quite as seriously as their lesbian sisters today. They stocked a surprising range of vibrators, butt plugs and other sex toys and also imported silicone, lesbian-friendly dildos from the States. Prior to this, if you had wanted to buy a dildo, you would either have to tiptoe furtively into Anne Summers or face the collective giggles of your gay brothers in shops like Clonezone or Zipper. Invariably, the only dildo available would be enormous, black, hideously veined and indubitably phallic – certainly not what we went through the feminist revolution for. But not everybody greeted the arrival of *Thrilling Bits* with delight.

> In the first issue of a British lesbian sex-toy company's catalogue, a dildo was named after me, as a form of sexual harassment. It was called 'The Sheila – the Spinster's best friend' in reference to the fact that my first book was called *The Spinster and Her Enemies*.[1]

This was, I suppose, taking product placement a little too far. The *Thrilling Bits* catalogue also sexually harrassed a well-known lesbian author with the 'Jeanette, the dildo for the cliteratti', and a well-known animal performer with 'Flipper', the dolphin-shaped dildo. *Thrilling Bits* may, as its co-owner Lisa Power admits, have been set up as a piece of mischief, but it certainly filled a hole in the lesbian market. Its success, including a sell-out stall at Pride that year, showed just how far lesbian attitudes to sex had changed.

Sheba Feminist Publishers followed the successful publishing of *A Restricted Country* with the first British collection of lesbian erotica, *Serious Pleasure*.[2] The Sheba Collective believed there were a large number of lesbians who, like themselves, wanted to read erotica written by lesbians for lesbians. And the Sheba Collective was right. There was a large number of lesbians 'out there' who did want to read lesbian erotica, but there was also a number of lesbians who did not. Cherry Smyth even considered using a pseudonym for her contribution to the collection, fearing that she would be denounced for the sex scene in her story 'Crazy for Mary Kelly'. But for her the book had an important function: '*Serious Pleasure* was about saying "if we feel so good about our bodies, why aren't we writing about it?" *Serious Pleasure* was not a betrayal of the past but an embracing of who we wanted to be and who we could be, if the thought-police would only relax.' The Sheba Collective had a clear notion of the politics that informed their collection.

> We see the collection as representing the diversity not only of our experiences and histories but of our desires and sexual practices. We do not label this approach as liberal; the differences within *Serious Pleasure* are framed by a feminist perspective which is informed by a radical approach to the politics of sex, race, class and culture. It is a perspective that celebrates the specifity of lesbian sexuality but does not see that sexuality as cut off from the rest of the world.[3]

Lesbian feminists did not accept the notion that a book like *Serious Pleasure* could be framed by any feminist perspective. Activist and writer Sue O'Sullivan had become something of a thorn in the flesh of lesbian feminism. Her opposition to Lesbians Against Sado-Masochism during the row at the London Lesbian and Gay Centre, and her writing, including her *Feminist Review* articles 'Upsetting an Applecart'[4] and 'Lesbian Summer of Love'[5] (both written with Susan Ardill) had left her labelled at best an 'apologist' for SM. As a member of the Sheba Collective, she was now branded a 'pornographer'. If the Sheba Collective had thought they might be able to engender some sort of debate about what is lesbian pornography or what is lesbian erotica, they were wrong.

For many lesbian feminists, of course, there was no difference. Pornography was pornography was pornography and
who was producing it for whom was totally irrelevant. Nor did
they see that something calling itself 'erotica' was any different
from pornography. Andrea Dworkin, the well-known American
anti-porn activist, just saw erotica as better produced porn for
a better sort of market. By this standard then, the stories in
Serious Pleasure are pornographic, but then so is virtually any
sexual activity.

The trouble was, however, that when it came to talking
about whether the book was pornographic or not, the actual
contents were rather irrelevant. From the moment that Sheba
asked for submissions for the collection, a sort of 'lesbian
whispers' had begun. Now, depending on who whispered what
to who, the message might be 'Sheba are going to publish
something really sexy', or 'Sheba are going to publish something utterly pornographic.' The bizarre result of this was that
on publication, the 'sexy' lobby found the collection somewhat disappointing and the 'pornographic' lobby found the
collection utterly pornographic. I attended one of the readings of *Serious Pleasure* in Manchester and my chief memories
were of the positive response that many women gave both the
contributors and the editors. Though some women did ask
pointed questions about pornography within the collection,
there was not the hysteria that had marked the showing of the
film *She Must be Seeing Things* the previous year. It is interesting to note, however, that the Grassroots Collective (who
then ran the book shop) had had much discussion as to
whether they would stock the collection at all.

The most 'controversial' contributions to the collection are
those by the British SM writer Barbara Smith. 'Masturbation

is for Wankers' is a witty exploration of one woman's rather haphazard experiences with a vibrator, while 'The Art of Poise' raises two rather knowing and ironic fingers to the lesbian feminist sisterhood.

> Am I really passive, objectified, unconsenting, deconstructed, feminine and known? Are you really active, male and annihilating? But something in me wants the tender touch that will destroy, the betrayer's kiss, the kiss-off. I want you to undo me, re-create me, open me up and out like the cliché rose.[6]

The truth about *Serious Pleasure* is that it is a sheep in wolf's bindings. The vast majority of stories show the protagonists as either in a relationship (but before the bed-death stage), or about to embark on some sort of long-term relationship, unless you count Amanda Hayman's story 'The Flame' – a sort of eco-feminist gang-bang. Only one story is set in the dangerously contentious realms of sexual fantasy ('A Visit to the Hairdressers') and there is little that is at all sexually 'dangerous' or 'daring' in the sex acts portrayed. There is virtually nothing that could be described as 'explicitly SM' and certainly nothing that could be said to 'degrade'. As a publishing company, Sheba always had the reputation of including women from different cultures and religions and experiences within its anthologies, *Serious Pleasure* is no different. Indeed, it is ironic that a book that was so attacked for its subject matter should far outstrip many other lesbian nonfiction and fiction anthologies in its efforts to include women from other cultures and religions.

What makes the collection different is how lesbian sex is

described. Up until the publication of *Serious Pleasure*, lesbian fiction had been dominated by romantic fiction and the burgeoning wave of lesbian detective fiction (which is romantic fiction with a dead body thrown in). Top of the romantic pops was the American publishing house Naiad Press. The Naiad scenario is simple: woman meets woman (one straight, the other not so sure after traumatic lesbian fumblings in girlhood); woman then has great sex with woman; lovers then have crisis that may ruin happy ever after; lesbians then live happy every after. In the wonderful world of Naiad, you can always be assured that the sex will be great, but you may be a bit bewildered by some of the sexual metaphors.

When her soft thighs opened to me I brushed the golden softness between with my lips, the most delicate softness of all, softer than the moss covering the earth beneath us, her moss damp to most gently stroking fingertips; within the moss the moist velvet flower of her . . .

. . . Blindly I pressed the throbbing center of me into the still-wet moss of her.

. . . Our bodies pulsing synchrony, I looked at her and fell into an endless depth of transparent blue . . .[7]

Yes, well, it's all very soft, mossy and velvety. The stories in *Serious Pleasure* are a far cry from the 'caressing her wetness' school of writing so quintessentially Naiad.

Then down to the pale blondish-coloured hair between Emma's thighs. She licked around the edges of Emma's cunt enjoying the musky smell and each gasp from Emma as she got close to the lip of her cunt . . . Then Alberta

sunk her tongue inside of Emma . . . She flicked her
tongue across the pointed hardness of Emma's clit. Then
drew it inside her mouth as she'd done Emma's nipple,
sucking it then pressing it between her teeth, gently, then
harshly, until Emma's body convulsed with the coming
orgasm.[8]

The photographer Jean Fraser describes *Serious Pleasure* as
being 'a democratisation of a new sexual language. Before if
you wanted to talk about lesbian sex, you were pigeon-holed as
SM, as somehow anti-feminist.' This is, perhaps, why the book
created so much opposition from lesbian feminist women.
Serious Pleasure, while not itself explicitly SM, gives a voice to
a new, more up-front sexuality that could certainly include
SM sex. Thus, its power is not so much about what it is as
what it represents. Books, like lesbian feminists, do not belong
in a vacuum. The publishing success of *Serious Pleasure*
showed that there was a significant body of lesbians who did
want to see their sexuality represented in a way that was
intensely sexual. I think it is too much to suggest that *Serious
Pleasure* created the spirit of the time, but it certainly caught it.
It is no surprise that Sheba followed its publication with a second collection, *More Serious Pleasure*. This collection is
slightly more adventurous than its predecessor, but is let down
by the quality of some of the stories included.

But can there ever be such a thing as lesbian porn or lesbian
erotica that can be acceptable to a lesbian feminist audience?
In the early 1980s, the lesbian photographer Tee Corinne produced a range of photographs that has been construed by some
feminists as lesbian erotica. Her series of photographs *Yantras
of Womanlove*[9] blends images of flowers with women's

genitals. Her picture 'Isis in the Woods' superimposes a photo of a labia on a peaceful woodland scene. It is part of a series of photographs which, as I remember, one American magazine described without any irony at all as 'labias in natural settings'. This type of photograph has gained some feminist approval.

> Some feminists did indeed create what they called a new kind of erotica. Tee Corinne is an example. In the service of validating the vulva she has photographed female genitals in landscape, on trees and on beaches. The association of the female genitals with natural forms, shells, flowers, fruits, has quite a long history in lesbian art. Such photographs are clearly a break with the traditions of male pornography where the vulva appears in order to stimulate the male to erection with thoughts of penetration. Women, it seems, can create art with sexual content which does not replicate male pornography.[10]

There are, of course, more interesting ways of 'validating the vulva' than looking at a fanny in a forest. Jeffreys' embracing of Corinne's work as lesbian erotica is questionable. Corinne's work is not all flowers and labias, her photographs picture women making love, fat women, women with disabilities, but these pictures are not overtly sexual, they are conceptual. Their primary role is not to display sex but the possibility of lesbian sexuality. They exist to validate the female, and indeed the lesbian, body. Sheila Jeffreys bemoans the fact that the lesbian erotica of the late 1980s and early 1990s is 'not about celebrating the beauty of the vulva', I'm not sure what would be particularly erotic about it if it did.

Anyway, by the late 1980s most of us had happily validated our vulvas, thank you very much. And as to celebrating them – I'll show you mine, if you show me yours.

The 'erotica' of Tee Corinne's work speaks to the politics and the time at which it was created. Throughout the 1980s in Britain, we saw how lesbians fought to change orthodoxies around lesbian sexuality. Thus the erotica of the late 1980s was bound to be very different to that of even a few years earlier. For some lesbian feminists the new erotic language of *Serious Pleasure*, with all its cunts and clits and fucks and fuckings, was just the same old oppressive erotic language of the heteropatriarchy. But other women began to argue that you could make a distinction between male-produced pornography and that produced by, and for, lesbians. It could be argued that the old arguments that porn is basically exploitative, or that it could be used to encite violence and rape, were no longer viable when it was clear that women, the usual victims of porn, were actually its consumers and its audience.

The publication of the first *Quim* magazine, in the summer of 1989, confirmed the arrival of a new brand of lesbian – the lesbian 'bad girl'.[11] She had actually been around for some time, but she had kept herself to the wicked world of clubs like Chain Reaction and the Clit Club. Branding itself as a magazine that wanted to 'talk about and celebrate what makes us lesbians – our sex with women', *Quim* deliberately placed itself in opposition to the lesbian feminist ideology that had gone before it.

Quim mirrors the great American sex lesbian magazine *On our Backs*. First published in 1984, *OOB* labelled itself 'Entertainment for the Adventurous Lesbian' and set itself against the long-standing radical feminist paper *Off our*

Backs, while shamelessly parodying its name. Its undoubted star was the sex radical Susie Bright, a.k.a Susie Sexpert.[12] Her regular column 'Toys for Us' was a witty compilation of sex advice, safe-sex tips and sexual-trend spotting. Each column would be accompanied by a photograph of Susie, sometimes sexy, sometimes ironic, often very funny. One of *OOB*'s other regular contributors was the British lesbian photographer Jill Posener. Posener is another of those nasty feminist traitors who has fallen from taking 'acceptable' photographs of lesbian political grafitti[13] to working for a sex magazine and being a strong opponent of pro-censorship lobbies in the States. *OOB* is deliberately provocative and it sets out to get up the noses of the feminist sisterhood, but it is written and photographed with an insouciance and irony that *Quim* lacked.

Quim was a serious sex magazine. And while it was published (like *Serious Pleasure*), because there were women out there who really wanted to read it, it was also an angry response to what the editors saw as the prescriptive lesbian feminism of the 1980s. It was a direct challenge to the sort of lesbian feminism that had led women to attack the lesbian SM club Chain Reaction with crowbars. Like *OBB*, *Quim* mixed photos with short stories, with non-fiction pieces and comments, though it was more overtly SM than its American counterpart. Over its five issues it covered a range of different subjects in its 'Quimquotes' (originally 'Cumquotes') section, including SM, butch and femme, and prostitution. In its last issue (Issue 5) *Quim* devoted a whole section to the voices of black women, addressing and acknowledging black women's sexuality in a way that no other magazine had tried or dared to do. On a more mundane level, it also asked women what they felt about their tits, cunts, how they come, how and if they masturbate. The magazine also championed, and indeed relied on, the work of photographers like Della Grace, Lawrence Jaugey-Paget and Lola Flash. Issue 4 contains a stunning collection of photographs, *Xenomorphisis*, by Della Grace. These photos seek 'to virtually deconstruct our notions of Woman, of Lesbian and of Perversion in order to create a space for the exploration and celebration of diversity and desire . . . *Xenomorphisis* is a gestation period in queer culture.' Grace is perhaps more convincing as a photographer than she is as a commentator on her own work, but the *Xenomorphisis* pictures suggested that the *Quim* editors had higher goals than just shocking their lesbian feminist detractors.

However, *Quim* always faced problems when it came to distribution. A number of bookshops, both inside and outside London, refused to stock the magazine.

> Well, children that we were, we naively expected that a lesbian magazine was going to be sold in lesbian and gay and women's bookshops – oh those heady days of sweet innocence. We were totally unprepared for the overwhelming censorship from within our own community.[14]

If, before its publication, those bookshops had been worried about the clear pro-sex, and therefore pro-SM, stance of the magazine, the first issue did nothing to allay their fears or make them wish to change their decision. Aside from the expected images of women in chains, in leather or in dog collars, there was one short story, a sexual fantasy about a nun and including sex with under-aged boys, that understandably caused much consternation.

The *Quim* editors also made it very clear what their editorial policy would be.

> So here's *Quim*'s bottom line. We are pro-sex full stop. We don't intend to cause offence, but we will never ever deny a woman's consensual sexual practices because another woman would rather she wasn't into what she's into. Straights are often disturbed when we kiss in the streets but if we'd kowtowed to the people who are offended by us we wouldn't be where we're at now.[15]

Quim defended its decision to print the story by stressing the fact that the story was sexual fantasy. Sophie Moorcock, one of *Quim*'s founding editors, defended the role of fantasy within lesbian sex in her article 'Drawing the Invisible Line'.[16] While she agrees that such fantasies are rooted in the oppression of a heterosexual society, she does not see the repression of these fantasies as the way to fight lesbian oppression. Neither does she believe that a fantasy life that involves either being sexually dominant or being sexually submissive will mean that that person is therefore either over-dominant or over-submissive in the reality of their daily life.

Unsurprisingly, Sheila Jeffreys has an altogether different view. For her 'what is fantasy today can be reality tomorrow'. She feels that the constant bombarding of the gay world with images of violence, fascism, etc. will eventually de-sensitise us all to the reality of oppression.

> I do not want to think that, when tanks and marching

boots and swastikas pass by in a real fascist coup, the gay
population will be experiencing a thud of erotic desire
which immobilises us.[17]

This is both an apocalyptic and patronising vision. Does
Jeffreys really think that those women who have rape fantasies
will automatically experience 'a thud of erotic desire' when
faced by an actual rapist? Isn't this dangerously close to affirming the notion that women actually enjoy being raped?

However, Issue 2 of *Quim* has a comment from the writer
Linda Devo. When asked if she has ever read a story that
turned her on but alarmed her, she replies,

> The Nun in the first issue of *Quim*. The part where the
> boys are being abused was really off to me but it was
> fantasy so that's ok.

The notion that absolutely anything can go as long as we call
it fantasy is as problematic as suggesting that sexual fantasy is
an inevitable part of violent reality.

The same issue then complicates matters further by including Trash White's story 'The Thief', where a 'sapphic virgin' is
raped by a lesbian cat-burglar.

> It's about being overpowered certainly but it's also about
> being pleasured which I think is what 'The Thief' is all
> about. The thief is able to empathise with what this other
> woman wants when she's partially submitting. It becomes
> a mutual [sic] and I think that women's fantasies about
> rape are subliminally consensual. A man would not be
> able to write a fantasy based on rape like that because

rape for them involves degradation. And pleasuring is
certainly not on their agenda.[18]

The above comment is awkward because it implicitly denies
the reality of lesbian rape. The problem is that only the perpe-
trator is allowed to decide what is pleasurable or not and we all
know where we've heard that one before. Trash White's notion
of consent in this context is equally unconvincing and changes
our reading of the short story. We can certainly read 'The
Thief' as fantasy and know that we don't have to worry about
notions of consent etc., but it is rather worrying to discover
that the author isn't bothered either. The subtle distinction
that men degrade, while women only pleasure, is not one that
survives scrutiny.

I could, of course, be just letting my lesbian feminist juices
flow when I quibble about *Quim*. As activist Liza Power says,
there is something 'naughty schoolgirl' about the magazine, it
dares you to be appalled. The message is that if you don't like
anything about it, then stop being such a tired old fuddyduddy
and go and read a Naiad. Sophie Moorcock writes that

> . . . we all have our personal preferences or limits but these
> will always be subjective and as specific as we are, and if
> we are not hurting anyone then no one – lover, friend,
> writer or bookseller – is ever entitled to tell us where those
> boundaries should be.[19]

It seems that *Quim* magazine was much happier to accept
those on the broadest part of the sexual spectrum than those at
its narrowest point. Not everybody is convinced by the 'anything goes as long as we are not hurting any one' approach.

The editors' declaration that they were 'pro-sex' leaves anyone who disagreed as 'anti-sex', and therefore just another shrivelled up lesbian prude. Whatever you think of the politics of all this, this unrelenting diet of red meat, unleavened by any vanilla, let alone any irony and humour, eventually makes the magazine rather hard-going. Perhaps this is why the later issues of *Quim* are more interesting – they seem much less about shocking the lesbian audience into submission and more about exploring complex sexual imagery. Of course it may just be that we had all got used to it. As anyone who has ever abandoned vegetarianism will know, a diet of red meat will initially send you running to the bathroom, but you soon get used to it.

It is true that if you didn't agree with *Quim* you didn't have to read it. But the early 1990s saw a new orthodoxy that trumpeted SM sexuality while at the same time decrying anything vanilla. Vanilla sex is basically the lesbian equivalent of the missionary position. It is sex that doesn't involve SM, role-playing, sex toys, fist-fucking, anal sex and anything else that you might consider a little risqué. It is assumed to be the sort of sex that lesbian feminists have – touchy, feely and only timidly penetrative. However, vanilla sex remains as undefined as SM, thus one woman's vanilla really can be another's SM. 1990s dykes solved this confusion by all deciding to look like SM dykes anyway, while keeping quiet about how much or how little SM or vanilla sex they were actually getting.

Indeed, 1990s clothes fashion amongst lesbians has followed our changing attitudes to lesbian sex. Lesbian sex radicals, following on the heels of such an ambivalent sexual personality as Madonna, have championed a new fashion for leather and rubber gear. At the same time, the early 1990s lesbian dress code of jeans, and Doc Marten boots and shoes has found a wider audience among heterosexual women. In the 1970s and 1980s, feminist and lesbian fashions marked women as clearly different from heterosexual norms. In the 1990s, it is interesting to see how many heterosexual women have adopted lesbian fashion and how a number of lesbians have re-adopted heterosexual female fashions. One result of the lesbian sex wars has been the return of the feminine looking (though not necessarily femme), lesbian. Like Madonna, the archetypal early 1990s role model, you never doubt that this woman is female but her fetish fashion and her dressing for sex make it clear she is in control of her own sexual power.

It is ironic that when the pro-sex lobby wrestled lesbian sexuality from the clutches of the lesbian feminists they also donned the mantle of the 'humourless' lesbian. This had previously been the proud domain of the lesbian feminists. In a world view that saw women's oppression at the root of everything, there was little time for a smile, a song or a dance routine (excepting, of course, those terrible lesbian feminist comedy troupes, ululating and circle dancing). By the 1990s, it was usual to see a lesbian comedienne taking the piss out of lesbian feminists, but woe betide you if you shifted your target to the pro-sex SM girls. There was nothing in the least bit amusing about genital jewellery, giving your partner an enema or having yourself 'crucified' at a lesbian sex club. SM was at the cutting edge and not the stuff of cheap jokes and easy innuendo. It is odd to think that SM could become just as much of an orthodoxy as lesbian feminism. And in this case, humour is an interesting illustration of who held the political upper hand. Lesbian feminism was an easy target of the lesbian comediennes because it had lost its political power, it was impossible to satirise the SM girls because they were at the cutting edge of late 1980s and early 1990s sexiness.

Of course, not all SMers would see it like that. Pat Califia, a sort of SM lesbian Judge Dredd, makes some great claims on behalf of SM. She seems to believe that lesbians will never truly love themselves until they get to grips with all aspects of their sexuality – most specifically the SM ones.

> Women – especially lesbians – exist under conditions that make us frightened to step out of line, frightened to challenge the status quo, almost unable to imagine what bold and brassy, peacock creatures we could be if we were free.[20]

If this weren't bad enough, of course, we are so oppressed by ourselves that we can't even describe our sexual practice accurately.

> It takes a lot of guts for lesbian writers to push beyond our anger about what women aren't allowed to do. We are prey to the suspicion that it's our fault and women don't deserve anything better. We are afraid of more opportunity because we might fail. This affects our ability to engender new (or at least accurate) sexual images that are genuinely exciting. The power of the censor within us is awesome.[21]

Califia tells us that if we are ever going to be free, we must have a vision of what 'sexy' means and what 'pleasure' means. While she has always been clear that it is SM that she thinks must be both 'sex' and 'pleasure', she is immensely dismissive of those who don't want to read about sex in the way she does: 'if you don't like to read about pussy maybe you don't like pussy and should be licking something else'.[22] Califia's assertion that somehow SM is the one true creed and that SM writing is the only way to write sex 'accurately' is irritating.

Califia's collection of short stories, *Macho Sluts*, is probably the most controversial of all collections featuring lesbian SM. It is not subtle or even always well written, but it's very shockability gives it a certain power. Califia plays around with notions of consent and sometimes dispenses with it altogether. Califia is not afraid to use gay men in her scenarios, indeed just about every sexual practice appears at some point in a Califia story. The stories are sometimes shocking, sometimes provoking and sometimes predictable. 'The Calyx of Isis' is an extraordinary encyclopaedia of SM sexual practice, featuring bondage, anal sex, fist-fucking, flagellation etc., etc., etc. It is meant to shock and it certainly does. More to the point, perhaps, it is utterly and deliberately pornographic.

However, while the stories in *Macho Sluts* can be read as a courageous attempt to push the boundaries of lesbian sexuality to absolute limits, it is odd that the introduction to the book suggests that all this has got to be good for you too. Califia is right to suggest that lesbians have censored themselves about sex, but the implication that somehow all lesbians writing about sex would have written SM if they only had the courage, is really rather daft. Certainly those who have chosen to write about sex in the ways that Califia or the *Quim* girls have done, have faced a tremendous barrage of criticism from those who oppose their views. A certain defensiveness in their writing is therefore understandable. However, what does not really work is to try and create a political ideology out of lesbian pornography. SM, like lesbian feminism before it, is no universal panacea. It is questionable whether the lesbian world will be truly liberated just by learning to pierce our partner's labia so that we can lace her cunt up.

But the publication of *Macho Sluts* in Britain was not as controversial as it might have been. It never, I believe, engendered the anger that *Coming to Power* had done nine years before. The lesbian political scene had changed enough to silence the voices of those who might have previously attacked it. While lesbian feminists and lesbian feminism had not gone away, it seemed to have stopped bothering to engage in the rows as once it had done. Attitudes and orthodoxies had, indeed, been altered.

Not that there wasn't the odd flurry of anger against the book. *Scene Out*, the Manchester-based lesbian and gay magazine, chose to ask a man to review Califia's book. This was deeply transgressive in the pre-queer North-west. So much so, indeed, that two anonymous lesbians placed a defamatory condemnation of both the book and the review on the notice board of the local alternative bookshop, telling lesbians not to read the book or buy the magazine. As a result, *Scene Out* threatened to sue the bookshop for allowing the letter to be displayed in the first place: an illustration not only that there was a caucus of women who still found such blatant SM totally unacceptable, but also that those who felt attacked were prepared to go to great lengths to fight off what they saw as attempts at censorship. The irony was that the bookshop had chosen not to sell the book anyway.

In London, the SM club Chain Reaction closed in 1990, but it was quickly replaced with a successor, The Clit Club.

Catering to a pro-sex SM crowd, the Clit Club became infamous for some of the 'sex scenes' performed live on its stage. Though it was highly trendy, not all women liked what they saw happening there. In an AIDS-conscious crowd, there were questions as to whether some of the 'sex scenes' in their desire to shock had not actually become dangerous and unsafe. Some women simply did not like the atmosphere and found that the need to be forever daring and shocking actually made the club chillingly predictable. Yet the Saidie Maisie Club at the London Lesbian and Gay Centre, which opened in 1991, seemed to be enjoyed by virtually everybody who visited it. Saidie Maisie's was the first mixed SM club. Jeni Bremner enjoyed it because

> It was incredibly friendly. Though the people who went took it seriously, they did not take it too seriously. As long as you yourself were comfortable, you could look how you wanted and be how you wanted. There was no pressure to be more shocking or more daring than anyone else.

The early 1990s and the rise of queer politics also brought a change in the way that some lesbian fiction writers began portraying lesbian life and life-style. The novels of the lesbian novelist and activist Sarah Schulman do not recreate the sunny, romantic world of the Naiad romance. In books like *After Delores* and *People in Trouble*,[23] the darker realities of lesbian relationships, jealousy, possessiveness, obsession are all grittily and realistically portrayed. Jane DeLynn's highly successful novel, *Don Juan in the Village*[24] is a gloomy recreation of one lesbian's search for lesbian happiness and love. As she stumbles from unsuccessful sex scene to disappointment and thwarted passion, DeLynn's anti-heroine could not be more different from the courageous heroines of lesbian romance. Interestingly, the way that both writers describe lesbian sex is quite different to much lesbian sexual writing. Not only is the writing anti-romantic, but it is also rather detached:

> She pressed her thumbs inside Molly, not like those girls who think their hands are substitute penises. She had technique. When Molly ate her, Sam leaned back on her knees as far as she could go. She knew how to accept pleasure.[25]

This new 'realism' in lesbian writing suggests a coming of age in how lesbians portray their sexuality. Romantic fiction exists as much to affirm lesbian identity as it does to create realistic portrayals of lesbian sexuality. In the world of the Naiad or its 1990s British equivalent, Silver Moon Books, the happy ending is always guaranteed. The novels of Schulman and DeLynn suggest that real life may not always be as simple. It is good that in the 1990s we are confident enough of our own sexuality to enjoy a mixed menu of lesbian fiction.

In little more than a decade, lesbian feminism has been kicked off the lesbian pedestal and SM put in its place. There are a number of different reasons for this. The very extremeness of the rows about sex in London in the mid- to late 1980s forced lesbians to take sides. That SM became such a huge issue for lesbians through disputes like that at the LLGC or the showing of *She Must be Seeing Things*, when it really didn't have to be, made the subsequent domination of SM strangely inevitable. Once some lesbians' desire to talk about lesbian sex in all its uncomfortable realities, whether that included SM, role-playing or even fantasy, became defined as being itself SM, a middle ground became very hard to fight for. Without sensible dialogue, no compromise could ever be possible. When *Quim* banged on about lesbian SM it was, in part, a defensive action. And in this case, defence really is much more attractive than attack. By talking up lesbian sex as being ever more dangerous, daring and subversive, it makes it much more interesting than sitting in a room talking about your political credentials.

The new embracing of SM was not just moved by defensiveness, it was also fuelled by a need to rebel. The late 1980s and early 1990s saw a new wave of lesbians arriving on the scene: younger, sassier and with a healthy sense of lesbian attitude. Since the movement was now reaching its early twenties (GLF and the WLM had been born in 1970), it was time for some more good old-fashioned teenage rebellion. And who better to rebel against than their lesbian feminist foremothers?

PART THREE

After the War is Over

Outside Influences

Thatcherism, Section 28, HIV and AIDS

The last thing you would expect of the average lesbian is that she could become a figure of fashion. But the lesbian of the 1990s is just that. Whether she is wearing her casual costume of jeans and Doc Martens or she is sporting the latest in fetish fashion or designer labels, she is the ultimate in fashionable chic. This is a far cry from the lesbian of the 1970s and early 1980s. She rejected fashion, calling it a heterosexist concept that restricted women's freedom. But in the 1990s, it is lesbians themselves who are making fashion happen. As lesbians have become more visibly sexualised they have become more visually interesting. When you see Top Shop filled with fetish fashions that have their roots in the SM clubs and on the pages of lesbian SM magazines, you know there really is danger in the air. But along with this flirtation with fashion has come a new spirit of commercialisation as lesbian politics lose their focus.

Lesbian and gay writers in the 1990s have commented on the growing commercialism of the lesbian and gay scene. We have long been used to the concept of the gay men's pink pound. The continuing success of lesbian sex-toy companies,

lesbian magazines, trendy lesbian clubs and even the proliferation of the fashion-conscious lesbian suggest that there may
be something akin to a lavender fifty pence out there. The
1990s consumerist lesbian could not be more different than the
1970s collectivist lesbian. This value change can be seen in
how we party and how we practise politics on the street and in
our bedrooms.

As the lesbian feminists put it, lesbianism does not exist in
a vacuum. And if how we live as lesbians has changed over the
last fifteen years, this is not just the result of our own internal
politicking but also of the influences of a wider society and a
wider politics.

Lesbian politics in the early part of the 1980s was still
greatly influenced by the ideas of collectivism and community
that had been a part of left-wing radical politics in the 1960s
and 1970s. Indeed, both the Gay Liberation Front (GLF) and
Women's Liberation embraced collectivist notions in their
approach to achieving their political ends. Organisations that
had grown out of the WLM were often organised through collective principles. Branches of Women's Aid, Rape Crisis,
Women's Centres, women's newsletters, bookshops, housing
schemes and even squats were run on collective lines.
Organisations were non-hierarchical, decisions were reached
through discussion and consensus, meetings were facilitated
and tasks were shared. The advantage of this approach was
that every woman was given a chance to participate in deci-
sion-making and have her voice heard.

Likewise, lesbian discos and women-only events were collective. Entry fees were charged but these were on a sliding
scale according to each woman's income, or dependent on
whether you were 'waged or unwaged'. Again the emphasis

was on including as many lesbians as possible. Efforts were also made to ensure that lesbians with disabilities or lesbians with children were not excluded from events. Women who became involved in organising conferences or open days were involved in long and earnest discussions about crèche facilities and adequate disabled access. They faced heavy criticism if these or any other facilities were not up to the mark. I remember one particularly successful conference where the organisers tempted fate by placing a complaints board at the exit. At the end of the day, the hundred or so women who attended had only one thing to say. 'There was no herb tea' was emblazoned furiously across the board.

For some of us, newly out in the Thatcher 1980s, there was something curiously frustrating about this 'Stop the Revolution, there is no herb tea' attitude of our lesbian sisters. This was the down-side of the collectivist approach. It seemed that every aspect of our organising had to be minutely discussed and exhaustively argued about and scrutinised. Small mistakes would be roundly criticised and unspoken rules could be all too easily broken. Some issues took up a disproportionate amount of our interest and attention. Crèches, which should have been a symbol of what was good about lesbian politics, became one of the most frequent causes of discontent. Should boy children be allowed to use them, and if they were allowed, at what age did they become too patriarchal to be allowed to play in them? Whilst we all called ourselves lesbians and all believed in the same goals, we did not always agree on how we should achieve them and consensus was often very difficult to achieve. Consensus, it was clear, took a lot of time and an awful lot of energy, not to mention an awful lot of subtle, and not so subtle, power play.

The growth of identity politics within lesbian feminism in the early to mid-1980s again stressed the need to give voice to all lesbians. However, it is arguable how successful the largely white lesbian movement has ever been at including black and Asian women and other women of different races and religions within its ranks. Evelyn Asante-Mensah, a black lesbian living in Manchester believes it was very hard for black women to work alongside white lesbians.

> Some white women wanted to be seen around black women because it gave them credibility and proved just how liberal they were. White women said they wanted to debate race issues with you, but it was very clear that they had little or no real understanding as to what these issues really mean. Some white women are so hung up about saying the right thing or doing the right thing that it becomes impossible for them to be themselves around you and then it becomes impossible for you to be yourself too.

Whilst efforts were made by lesbians to ensure disabled access to events and/or provide signers, disabled lesbians too could feel excluded from the lesbian community. As one disabled lesbian told me, 'Whenever lesbians think of us, they think of us in terms of disabled access or special facilities, they don't seem to be able to comprehend that we are people too. They never really seem to look beyond what they see as our disabilities.'

Likewise, working-class women could feel excluded from a movement that, in theory, encouraged their participation and welcomed their experiences. Often lesbian discussion groups or organisations were dominated by very vocal, white middle-class women. It was easy to trip up by using right-off language or wearing the wrong sort of clothes or too much make-up. However, lesbian groups at this time could also be amazingly empowering and exciting. They often provided an easy and accessible social life where it didn't matter what you wore or what you looked like (as long as you didn't wear lipstick). The vegetarian lesbian in her earnest discussion group remains the butt of many a 1990s lesbian joke, yet some of us forget that we actually came out in groups like these or know many women who did.

The lesbian feminist movement had been largely influenced by the separatist principles. It was believed that women living and working together without the influence of men would be able to overturn patriarchal power. Many lesbians had chosen to live their lives completely separately from men, moving out of cities and towns to live in separatist communes and collectives. However, as the 1980s progressed, it became very difficult for many women to sustain that separatist energy. Some women simply burnt out, exhausted by the effort and the many criticisms they had often faced from other lesbians. Others felt it was time to change their lives and move on. For some women, growing inflation, and the economic boom and bust made it financially very difficult to maintain their separatist life-styles. It was also clear that the 1980s generation of lesbians, some of whom had enjoyed the separatist energy of Greenham Common, did not have the will to keep the separatist energy going either.

At the same time, many of the organisations that had traditionally employed lesbians, or where lesbians provided the impetus and the energy, were beginning to feel the economic bite. Organisations like Women's Aid and Rape Crisis had often relied heavily on the financial support of their local authorities. As the 1980s progressed, even the staunchest left-wing authorities were beginning to feel the strain as Tory central government tightened the financial screw. Women's organisations, drop-ins, women's centres and other voluntary organisations either were forced to go it alone or shut their doors, and it became much harder to find financial support for your conference or your women-only disco. The vicious destruction of the GLC in London in 1986 spelled the end of many small organisations that had provided support, and indeed employment, to many lesbians. Most importantly, perhaps, these economic pressures put paid to many of the networks (both formal and informal) that lesbians had established. Many lesbians began to look for work, out of necessity, beyond the sphere of these sorts of voluntary organisations.

Though they had been largely limited to London, the arguments about lesbian sexual practice that characterised the mid-1980s did have a major effect on the wider lesbian politics at the time. Old alliances had been broken and arguments had left uncomfortable scars. Some women began to feel out of touch with lesbian politics and disenchanted with the changes they saw around them. The incredible energy and excitement that women's politics had engendered in the 1970s had largely disappeared by the mid-1980s. Fewer and fewer women were shouldering more and more responsibility for the movement with less and less time to give.

The lesbian feminist movement, and the many social groups and organisations that had sprung up around it, were also extremely dependent on the efforts and energies of what was often a very small pool of women. This was particularly true of the lesbian groups that existed outside of London. By the

1980s, many of these women were simply tired and were looking to a new generation of lesbians to pick up the mantle of
organising for a lesbian community. Without the support of
local authority funding and, most importantly, without the
will to organise in the same lesbian feminist ways, this new
generation found other things to occupy its mind.

Indeed, lesbians were not immune from the individualistic
1980s. Why shouldn't lesbians own their own homes or drive
their own cars? The collective, with its constant effort and its
constant discussion, was to seem less and less appealing as the
1980s progressed. Newer lesbians coming on the scene by the
late 1980s and early 1990s had hardly experienced any other
politics than those of Thatcher and the monetarist Right. The
power of the patriarchy was far less alluring than the power of
the pound. Lesbians could be as fashionable and as glamorous
as their gay brothers or their straight sisters; why should they
stay in boring discussion groups when everybody else was out
there partying? This did not mean that younger lesbians could
not be political, it is just that they had different goals and different aspirations, and their politics was informed by a vastly
different society.

Indeed, it is arguable that some of the late 1980s conflicts
about lesbian sex and sexuality were, at their core, really the
arguments of two differing generations of lesbians with very
differing experiences. Young or new lesbians on the scene in
the 1980s might never have felt as oppressed by patriarchy as
their feminist sisters. The very success of feminism at bringing
women into new careers and challenging old patriarchal
orthodoxies about women's place in the home or in society,
distanced a new, younger generation of lesbians from these old
realities and experiences. For one generation, SM could only

ever be a reflection of violent patriarchal male society. For another, seeing lesbianism not as a political response to male power but as a positive sexual choice in itself, SM could be a perfectly valid lesbian sexual practice.

The 1980s also saw a new and powerful attack on lesbian and gay rights. In 1987, Lord Halsey sponsored a bill in the House of Lords banning the 'promotion of homosexuality', though this was initially rejected, the bill was to reappear not long afterwards in the form of the notorious Clause 28 (later Section 28) of the Local Government Bill. Clause 28 galvanised a whole new generation of lesbians and gay men into political action. Clause 28 prohibited any local authority from 'intentionally promot[ing] homosexuality or publish[ing] material with the intention of promoting homosexuality', neither was there to be any teaching of the acceptability of homosexuality 'as a pretended family relationship'. This extraordinarily spiteful and small-minded piece of legislation remains on the statute today, although it has never been tested in a court of law. Quite what a 'pretended family relationship' actually is or how one 'promotes homosexuality' remains open to question, but the power of Section 28 lies in the way that it allows local authorities to censor lesbian and gay activities and bullies lesbians and gay men into censoring themselves.

For many lesbians and gay men, this piece of anti-gay legislation came startlingly out of the blue. It had been a little over twenty years since homosexuality had been decriminalised and many lesbians and gay men had concentrated their activism subsequently on working with left-wing local authorities and within the Labour Movement where they had made many positive advances. It was their success in using

Equal Opportunities to champion lesbian and gay rights that, ironically, led to the introduction of Section 28. The Labour Party's support of lesbian and gay issues and the decision of a number of high-profile left-wing local authorities to be seen to be actively supporting of lesbian and gay rights was perceived as something of a vote-winner for the Tory Right. Section 28 was designed as a vindictive tool to slap down 'loony left' local councils. However, the Right certainly did not expect the major result of the introduction of Section 28. Simply, Section 28 changed the whole tempo of gay activism in the 1980s. Anti-Section 28 groups grew up in cities and towns throughout Britain, national organisations like the Organisation of Lesbian and Gay Action (OLGA) led the fight against the section, while rallies and conferences were held in London, Brighton, Manchester and Edinburgh. Though Section 28 was not defeated, the lesbian and gay movement learnt some vital lessons in campaigning and lobbying which paved the way for the 1990s activist groups, Outrage! and Stonewall.

I believe that Section 28 also had a particular significance for lesbian activists and the many younger or new lesbians fresh to the political scene. Though Section 28 did not refer to lesbians overtly, the nasty jibe about 'pretended family relationships' hit directly at the many lesbian mothers and mothers-to-be in the lesbian and gay community. Section 28 also made it clear that in the eyes of the law, lesbians could be actively and equally as nasty as their gay brothers: Section 28 was clearly designed to be an equal opportunities piece of bigotry. The lesbian response to Section 28 was as angry and active as the gay men's. Indeed, lesbians were to play a major and highly active part in much of the campaigning against the section. Indeed it was a group of lesbians who were to organise and carry out the two most exciting actions of the Section 28 campaign. First, a group of lesbians successfully abseiled into the House of Commons, thus creating national publicity for the campaign. They followed this with an hilariously successful attack on the BBC's Six O'Clock News when Sue Lawley (never the staunchest supporter of gay rights) and Nicholas Witchell were 'invaded' by lesbians. No piece of lesbian and gay direct action before or since has never matched this for sheer effrontery and gall. Never have lesbians been more gloriously visible.

The notion that lesbians and gay men could work very successfully together was certainly not a part of the lesbian feminist orthodoxy. Lesbian feminists were deeply suspicious of gay men, criticising their life-style and more particularly their sex-style and making it clear that they were equal players in patriarchy's oppression of women. Many lesbians, whilst fully understanding that years of equal opportunities training did not stop gay male activists being sexist, realised that Section 28 was serious enough to demand that lesbians and gay men did at least try to work and campaign together. This was not always very easy. The disintegration of the highly successful North-West Campaign for Lesbian and Gay Equality was as much due to the massive gulfs between gay men and lesbians as it was about the conduct of one of its officers. When the publicity officer of the campaign admitted to having once recruited for the National Front, it was the fact that the mainly male committee had known about it all along that most incensed the lesbians, many of whom formed their own splinter group Women Against Section 28.

However, meetings and conferences about Section 28 could

be frustrating affairs. I remember one conference in Strathclyde, organised in seconds, where the lesbians arrived to discover there was no designated women-only space. Some lesbians complained, a space was duly arranged and off we all trotted. There then followed a rather pointless discussion about the fact that there had been no women-only space. In sheer frustration a couple of us pointed out that we were there to discuss what we would do about Section 28. Silence followed. Other conferences and rallies had to deal with such dangerous issues as whether gay men should be allowed to staff the crèche or whether there would be a woman-only social. This all seems somewhat ludicrous now, but a lot of time both before, during and after Section 28 was spent worrying over such issues. Many of us began to feel that they were often allowed to obscure what we were actually trying to achieve. Some lesbians and gay men believed that Section 28 signalled the beginning of a new campaign against homosexuality that would lead inevitably to the labour camps. Amidst all the apocalyptic talk, one gay man once wearily turned to me and asked if we would want a women-only space in ours.

At the heart of these arguments lay the very different approach that some lesbians had to politics and political activism. Lesbian feminism had turned the lesbian gaze very much upon the lesbian community. Arguments about lesbian sexual practice, whether they be about fancying, role-playing, lesbian pornography or SM, had focused lesbian minds on putting our own, lesbian house, in order. Section 28 was a vivid and frightening illustration that the real enemies of lesbianism were not those lesbians who practised SM, they were the bigots and the homophobes. Once Section 28 became law, there was little doubt that other, more damaging laws would follow. This is not to say that lesbian feminists were not very active and powerful voices in the campaign – many were. It was just that the time for lengthy and torturous discussions was over. This 'luxury' would have to be put on hold while active campaigning was prioritised. It was also very clear that since bigots did not bother about arguments about crèche facilities, lesbians and gay men had to be pragmatic and change their own styles of campaigning and communicating to challenge homophobia.

Campaigning against Section 28 was also a lot more exciting than whining about whether there was a women-only space or not. For many younger or new to the scene, lesbians who had not been part of Women's Liberation or who had missed the growth of lesbian feminist politics, Section 28 provided a deeply exciting and empowering climate for political action. To be a part of a movement that has a fixed goal and a justifiable anger fuelling it, is a marvellous feeling and a whole new generation of activists was born. Although Section 28 did become law, the anger and power of the lobby that opposed it has ensured that the feared onslaught of anti-gay and -lesbian legislation has not yet appeared.

Section 28 brought many lesbians and gay men together in an active lesbian and gay politics. The political separatism of lesbians and gay men that had marked the early 1980s had certainly been eroded. This did not mean that lesbians and gay men had not mixed socially in the 1970s and 1980s. In small towns and cities lesbians and gay men could not avoid meeting each other in the single gay bar or club that might exist in the town. Although lesbians, if they were lucky, could save their real nights out until the once-a-month or once-a-week women-only discos. Other mixed gay clubs even had their own

women-only spaces. In the late 1980s, Rockies in Manchester
ran a small women-only disco, Radclyffe's, usually referred to
as the Well of Loneliness by all the gay boys. Certainly you
would have been very unlikely indeed to see a separatist lesbian
in a venue like that. When lesbians today criticise the lack of
separation between lesbians and gay men that we see in the
1990s, it is important to remember that this isn't altogether
new. What lesbians have lost, it can be argued, is both the will
and the financial power to organise socially on their own. But
more of that later.

Tragically, the 1980s were also to see the beginnings and
indeed the spread of a terrible new disease, AIDS. Many lesbians became involved in the fight against the disease
whether as carers or campaigners. The effects of HIV and
AIDS on the lesbian and gay communities in Britain have
been enormous. Friends, family, lovers and partners have all
been lost to the disease. Gay men have been the easy scape-
goat for a disease that is spread through sex and not sexuality
and all of us have felt the increased wave of homophobia that
the disease has brought with it. AIDS has also brought with
it a new anger within the lesbian and gay community. The
success of direct action group, Act Up, with its clear message
'Silence = Death' showed that lesbians and gay men were not
going to sit down and let the government ignore them while
the disease spread. This direct action activism, involving 'die-
ins' and highly vocal protests, was aimed directly at the
people who ignored the plight of gay men or who fostered
homophobia against us.

HIV and AIDS pulled sex into the public arena. The 1980s
saw an incredible proliferation in discussion about sex and sexual practice. The condom became one of the major symbols of

the decade. This did not always sit very easily with a Tory government's desire for a return to Victorian values. Sex, safe but non-reproductive, was promulgated as a way of ensuring a nation's healthy future.

For lesbians, HIV and AIDS have brought many issues about lesbian sexuality to the surface. In the early days, lesbians were assumed to be on the margins of the HIV debates and their sexual practices were seen as intrinsically safe. However, that suggests that all lesbians share the same sexual behaviours and that there must therefore be one sort of sexual practices that we can all call lesbian sex. The lesbian sex wars clearly showed that lesbians cannot provide one set of definitions about what lesbian sex might or might not be. There is still a massive amount of confusion and uncertainty about what concepts like 'safe sex' or 'low risk' really mean for lesbians.

> From the early years of the epidemic, when lesbians tended to wax lyrical about the safeness of lesbian sex, to the later period of assertions about the necessity of safer sex for everyone, to the present point of fracture and disagreement, there has never been a collective sense of what HIV means for lesbians. Today, some are saying that safer sex for lesbians is a red herring: it detracts from the real ways lesbians are affected by HIV and obscures the need for safer-sex education and practice in the communities and groups who are really at risk. Others say that this position is irresponsible: no one knows for sure if the virus can be transmitted by oral sex, for instance, and it is better to be safe than sorry. Still others, including some positive lesbians, are convinced that lesbian sexual

transmission had already happened and may happen more if lesbians don't practice safer sex now.[1]

Whatever lesbians believed about risk of transmission of HIV and AIDS, it is clear that it would be very difficult to discuss the concept of safe sex until lesbians began to talk more openly about their sexual practice and sexual behaviour. How much this has happened is open to debate. Jeni Bremner, formally HIV co-ordinator for a London Borough, and a well-known trainer on sexuality issues, believes that discussions about safer sex have helped some lesbians to talk about their sexuality more openly. 'Lesbian sex is hardly ever talked about by lesbians', she says. 'For some lesbians, safe-sex discussions have shown them that their sexual practices are not out of the ordinary or somehow non-lesbian. These practices have names.' Certainly in the 1990s many lesbians are much more upfront about what they want from sex and from their sexual partners.

AIDS educators quickly learnt that pictures of icebergs were not necessarily the most effective way of spreading a safe-sex message. Clever slogans might make a political point but it was up-front and sexy imagery that would really get the safe-sex message across. Gay pubs and clubs became saturated with a potent new imagery of male sexuality, through poster campaigns sponsored by AIDS charities and the Health Education Authority. Consciously or unconsciously, lesbians too were soaking up these pro-sex images: there really was little time for prudery when people were becoming ill around you. Indeed, images that once would have been considered pornographic were allowable when presented in the context of safe sex. The gradual assimilation of SM as a valid, and indeed permissible, form of lesbian sexual practice has been part and parcel of this change. The emphasis that SM places on notions of consent, and indeed safety, ties in neatly with a pro-sex, safe-sex consciousness. At the same time, the pro-sex imagery that abounded in lesbian and gay pubs and clubs, in safe-sex leaflets, or on posters, could also be seen in the sexy and provocative fashions that lesbians began to favour.

However, there have also been great disagreements between lesbians and gay men about lesbians and HIV. Some gay men have argued against time or money being given towards lesbians and HIV when they are clearly at such a low risk. Some men have wilfully ignored the contribution that lesbians have made to supporting those with HIV whether as volunteers or health professionals, friends or family. Lesbians have challenged gay men about their attitudes to women's health issues. Jeni Bremner packs no punches when she says 'I have no doubt that had AIDS affected lesbians instead of gay men, we would never have seen the gay men taking such an active and committed role in combating the disease and supporting its victims. They would still have been in the clubs partying.' Other women have pointed out that the incidence of breast cancer amongst lesbians is significantly high, yet little or no support or priority is given to researching incidence in the disease among lesbians.

The 1990s have seen lesbians asking new questions about lesbian health issues as AIDS and HIV have opened women's eyes to the importance of our sexual health. It is often very difficult for lesbians to discuss their health issues with a heterosexual doctor. In London two clinics – the Sandra Bernhard and the Audre Lorde – deal specifically with lesbian health issues. There are still too many doctors who either quiver with embarrassment at the very mention of lesbianism or who scarcely hide their disapproval. There is also much confusion about the risk to lesbians of cervical cancer. Many women are deeply concerned when doctors blithely assure them that they are not at risk of cervical cancer, without ever bothering to ask if they might have a heterosexual past. That both the Audre Lorde and the Sandra Bernhard clinics exist at all, tells us something about how our attitudes to lesbian health and, indeed, our sexual health have changed and how poorly our health issues have been treated in a heterosexual health service.

Lesbians might not feel that their sexual practices may make them vulnerable to HIV transmission, but this does not mean they are not vulnerable to other sexually transmitted diseases such as herpes or chlamydia. Lesbians also, of course, sleep with men and may inject or have injected, drugs intravenously. The need to be aware of safe-sex issues has meant that lesbians have become much more open in their analysis of other lesbians' sexual practices.

The 1990s have brought an increase in information for lesbians about sexual practice and sexual health. Prior to this, lesbians had to either rely on Pat Califia's ground-breaking guide *Sapphistry*,[2] the earlier and pretty awful *Joy of Lesbian Sex*,[3] or the more gung-ho writings of the American lesbian therapist JoAnn Loulan. Loulan sells the idea of a happy lesbian sex life like other people sell double glazing. In books like *Lesbian Sex*[4] and *Lesbian Passion*,[5] she demystifies lesbian sex as well as dealing with many lesbian sexual problems, all with the zeal of a practiced saleswoman. Whilst Loulan is refreshingly honest and up-front about lesbian sexuality, her very enthusiasm can leave you breathless and exhausted. Both she and Susie Bright, the other very fine sexual communicator, share an honesty about lesbian sexuality and a skill at confronting lesbian sexual taboos, both of them have been way ahead of any British writers.

Aside from the up-front discussions of lesbian sex that could be found in the British *Quim* magazine, British lesbians have taken a lot longer to find the courage to produce lesbian sex information, in either video or book form. The 1993 video *Well Sexy Women* combines a round-table discussion about sexual practice with a number of filmed sexual 'scenes', including such sexual practices as vanilla sex, fist-fucking, cunnilingus, anal sex and sex toys. Not all these filmed sex scenes work. A scene when one lover tries to excite her partner by masturbating in front of her led one woman I know to exclaim 'What's she doing, playing the ukelele?' The juxtaposition of lesbian chit-chat and up-front sex is not always a comfortable one. Is the message of the video really about safe sex and sexual practice or is it the opportunity to see some graphic lesbian sex in the guise of a lesson in safe sex and sexual practice?

Likewise, *Making Out*,[6] the latest lesbian sex guide, marries an informative text with a series of what the jacket describes rather tweely as 'fantasy narratives'. (Oh, where oh where were the speech bubbles?) These 'fantasy narratives', as the phrase suggests, bear absolutely no relationship to the text, and whilst they are a massive improvement on the coy old pen and ink drawings that previous lesbian sex books used, you can't help wondering what they are doing there. Some of Jaugey-Paget's photography is superb, her photos of two black lesbians, one heavily pregnant, are both highly sensitive and highly original. Schramm-Evans' text is serious and informative. I do wonder however, what the anti-SM brigade would make of this particular sentence: 'The term sadist is a very loaded one these days, and is rarely used in the SM scene as it carries connotations of abuse and non-consenting violence.'[7] They might be surprised to discover that their SM sisters are so sensitive. Both *Making Out* and *Well Sexy Women* show how lesbian attitudes to sex have changed in the 1990s. Both are influenced by the need to talk about sex openly and both use clear pro-sex and up-front sexual imagery. Yet a certain unease remains. Lesbians in the 1990s can be fed images of lesbian sexuality if it is educational, they can be fed images if they are lesbian SM, but there is nothing much else in the middle.

The 1980s saw the increasing sexualisation of lesbians and lesbianism. This was created within the lesbian movement itself as lesbians sought to discuss all aspects of their sexuality in their search for a lesbian sexual identity. We have seen how arguments about lesbian sexuality and lesbian sexual practice themselves created the energy for a more up-front, pro-sex lesbian sexuality. This coincided with a new openness about sexual practice as safe sex became one of major lesbian and gay responses to HIV and AIDS. Many lesbians are very uncomfortable about what they see as a modern-day obsession with sex and sexual practice. Lesbian feminism may no longer be our major political orthodoxy, but many lesbians, by the end of the 1980s, were questioning the pro-sex lobbies' wholesale rejection of many of the things that feminism had stood for. Most particularly, into the 1990s we have seen the depoliticising of lesbianism continue. Where once we had a political choice around lesbianism, we have now got what we call a lifestyle choice. Lesbianism is now available 'off the peg', where once it was a highly tailored political idea shaped to match the needs of a political ideology.

The 1980s have also seen the beginnings of the backlash against the feminism of the 1960s and 1970s. While we are constantly being told that we have achieved some sort of equality with men, we are still aware that we are consistently under-paid for what we do and are still under-represented in the higher echelons of business, let alone within the establishment and within government. Feminism is also regularly blamed for all sorts of ills, not least the break down of the nuclear family.

Lesbians too have had their own lesbian backlash. Lesbian sex wars and other arguments about sex and sexual practice have fuelled a powerful, and often destructive, backlash against our lesbian feminist sisters and feminism itself. We may not have always agreed with their ideas about sex and sexuality, we may have questioned their definitions of lesbianism and lesbian sex, but we should not let these disagreements wipe out the achievements that lesbian feminism and feminist activity have wrought. Without the first generation of out lesbian activists there could be no second. Many of the things we now take for granted on the scene, whether they be bookshops, phonelines or even the latest trendy club, have their roots in lesbian and feminist movements that saw the vital need to provide lesbians with their own spaces and their own facilities. It was this generation of lesbians that taught us that we could genuinely be proud of who we are.

The 1980s was a decade of extraordinary change for lesbians and for lesbian sexual politics. Within the somewhat narrow confines of lesbian politics, lesbian sex was fought over and argued over. At the start of the decade sexual practices like butch and femme, role-playing and SM were decried. By the decade's end they were accepted and approved of. At the same time the influences of Thatcherism brought an end to the collective energy of the lesbian political movement as individualism became the byword. Section 28 brought a new generation of lesbian and gay activists out on to the streets while at the same time allowing lesbians the opportunity to re-evaluate the politics that had gone before. Indeed, the political gaze moved away from internal politics of lesbian feminism to a wider political arena. HIV and AIDS encouraged lesbians to think again about their attitudes to lesbian sex as they came to terms with a new visual and verbal language of sex. Lesbians and gay men began to work together both against Section 28 and in the lesbian and gay response to the arrival of HIV and AIDS.

The destruction of part of the lesbian and gay infrastructure, which came with the closure of the GLC and the end of local authority support of lesbian and gay facilities, has hastened the new commercialism we see in 1990s lesbian and gay living. As lesbian discos or lesbian-only spaces have been removed, lesbians and gay men have worked together to create lesbian and gay spaces, clubs and bars. In cities like Edinburgh, Glasgow, Manchester and London the 1990s have seen the creation of lesbian and gay cafe culture. How much this new commercialism excludes as well as includes has yet to be established.

The 1990s maintains this new commercialism and lesbians and gay men are moving closer together both politically and socially. The 1990s have also seen a challenge to old lesbian and gay orthodoxies as a new sort of politics has grown in the lesbian and gay movement. Queer politics bring lesbians and gay men firmly into the 1990s. Queer art and culture, queer fashion and activisism, and even queer sex, has splashed homosexuality firmly into the heterosexual consciousness. What queer has to say for lesbians and lesbian sexuality is another story.

Of Quims And Queers

Polymorphous perversity and the new dildocracy

If in the 1980s the typical dyke about town owned a cat and a bicycle, her 1990s sister seems much more likely to possess a dog and a dildo. The dildo, reviled by lesbian feminism as a tool of the patriarchy, has now become a potent symbol of lesbian sexuality. It has also become a totem for the new queer sexuality, a sexuality which, at its best, both challenges and subverts.

Madonna was the public face of queer in the early 1990s. Her 1990 hit 'Justify my Love' was itself both blatant and raunchy, but it gained further notoriety with an accompanying video which contained a lesbian sex scene. The video was immediately banned by the BBC, ensuring that the record became a huge hit. Madonna has continued to play around with notions of women's sexuality; she can be both powerful and vulnerable, victim or virago. Her coffee-table book *Sex*[1] was both a tribute to her monstrous ego and to her skill at flouting the rules about how women should express themselves sexually. She has also flirted very openly with her lesbian sexuality, whether by hanging around gay bars with her friend Sandra Bernhard or by openly admitting a lesbian relationship in 1994. But in a lesbian world eager for an icon, Madonna remains an uneasy one. Is she genuinely 'queer' or is she merely a practised opportunist? Does she really challenge patriarchal assumptions about women's sexuality or does she merely pander to them? What Madonna does succeed in doing is using the sexual coinage of SM and lesbian sexuality to display women's sexual power and ability to make their own sexual choices. Love her or hate her, she is a potent symbol of how the trappings of a sexual minority can be used to challenge a sexual majority. It is this challenge that queer epitomises, both as sexuality and as politics.

The end of the 1980s saw a new type of lesbian and gay activist arriving on the scene. No longer willing to accept meekly whatever straight society threw at them, they decided to take their politics right to the doors of their oppressors. The formation of the AIDS direct action group ACT UP was followed by the birth of a new 'queer nation' politics and the creation of the British lesbian and gay direct action group, Outrage! This was the new 'queer' politics. Queer was to provide not only a potent force for lesbian and gay activism but was to impact deep into the lesbian and gay community. Queer has changed many of our perceptions of our sexuality as well as providing a vital intellectual force in the Arts and Academia.

This new 'queer' activism took its name from the American direct action group Queer Nation. Queer, itself, had long been a pejorative description of male homosexuals, but queer activists reclaimed the word and turned it from an insult into a powerful statement of activism and involvement. With slogans like 'Queer as fuck' and 'We're here, we're Queer, get used to it', lesbians and gay men effectively subverted language, turning bigoted insults into powerful statements of lesbian and gay power and anger. Whilst the queer struggle and the politics of Outrage! retain many of the same goals as other political groups (for example Stonewall), by seeking to end discrimination against lesbians and gay men and promote our basic human rights, its approach and style could not be more different.

Queer politics are structured around the notion that activism should be 'in your face'. This is not an assimilationist vision but is founded on the notion that it is straight society that will have to change its ideas and its attitude towards lesbians and gay men before lesbians and gay men change themselves to fit in with straight society. Mere tolerance or acceptance of homosexuality is not enough. Lesbians and gay men should not have to 'normalise' themselves to find their place in a wider society; rather society should 'queer' itself up first. Whilst Stonewall, the lesbian and gay political lobbying group, relies on building partnerships and links with the establishment to create political change, Outrage! uses the power of anger and publicity to force a societal change. 'In your face' activism demands a high media profile for lesbian and gay action specifically because it makes homosexuality the issue.

Outrage! was formed in Britain in 1990 by a group of gay activists led by Peter Tatchell. Many lesbians went to the early meetings at the Gay Centre and joined the early Outrage! events including a kiss in at Piccadilly, followed by a Queer wedding in Trafalgar Square. Outrage! worked by setting up a number of different affinity groups, each concentrating their energies on specific targets. Thus the Whores of Babylon (Queers fighting Religious Intolerance) were to lead many sorties into the pulpits of homophobic churches, and SISSY

(Schools Information Services on Sexuality) caused much controversy, and indeed publicity, when it handed out pro-gay leaflets at a London secondary school. PUSSY (Perverts Undermining State Scrutiny) was both feminist and anti-censorship and challenged state, and indeed lesbian, censorship. It included some of the women who were members of the more sedate Feminists Against Censorship (FAC) as well as some of the gay men from Outrage! Most importantly, PUSSY also wanted to dispel the myth that lesbianism was more about politics than it was about sexual choice or sexual activity.

Although the anti-pornography movement in Britain never quite reached the heights of the campaigns led by MacKinnon and Dworkin in the States, 1991 saw an attempt by the labour MP Dawn Primarolo to introduce the Locations of Pornographic Materials Bill. This would have restricted the sale of all pornographic materials to strictly licensed shops. While its promoters presented the bill as acting in the interests of all women and being inspired by the best feminist intentions, PUSSY opposed the bill because they saw how it would be used to limit the sale of all lesbian and gay materials, pornographic or not, and might even be used to limit the distribution of safe-sex information. Indeed, a similar piece of anti-pornography legislation in Canada in 1992 did result in an alternative bookshop being prosecuted for selling the lesbian sex magazine *Bad Attitude*.[2]

PUSSY was also influential in challenging what they saw as the censorship, by certain bookshops, of the British lesbian sex magazine *Quim*. At the same time, Della Grace's book *Love Bites*[3] faced similar problems of distribution within lesbian and gay bookshops, although, oddly, it was widely sold throughout Waterstones and Dillons. PUSSY not only made every effort to promote both the magazine and Grace's book, but also challenged bookshops to explain why they could not, or did not wish to, stock the book or magazine. Silver Moon did stock *Quim* but hesitated about selling *Love Bites* as it felt that one of the images of a lesbian being fucked from behind by a dildo-wearing dyke might bring them into conflict with the Obscene Publications Squad. Sisterwrite, the more right-on feminist bookshop, refused to stock either the magazine or the book because the collective felt that both were porno-graphic and therefore anti-women. Gays the Word, the London lesbian and gay bookshop, refused to stock Grace's book but never seemed particularly clear why. Frontline Books in Manchester (formerly, Grassroots) held to its policy of not selling any material that might be defined as pornographic, lesbian or not. This is a stance that it keeps to this day. Only the lesbian and gay bookshop West and Wilde in Edinburgh never had a worry about selling *Quim* or *Love Bites*.

PUSSY responded to what it saw as censorship of lesbian sexual material by organising various actions and pieces of street theatre outside the London bookshops. At the same time they also tried to broaden the debate on lesbian sex and cen-sorship by organising a highly successful open forum with contributors and contributions from many of the organisa-tions involved. PUSSY also made great efforts to sell *Quim* magazine wherever possible. They did not want to see this magazine, which always struggled against the economic odds, failing because certain bookshops could not bring themselves to stock it.

PUSSY also worked to raise the profile of the case of Jenny White who attempted to take the Customs and Excise Department to court after it seized some lesbian sex videos she had bought whilst in America. Although she knew she was not going to win her case, she did not have to pay costs which she regarded as a minor victory in the face of state censorship. What made the case bizarre was that a couple of the films had already been shown in independent cinemas in Britain.

A new affinity group grew in Outrage! at the time of the prosecution of Jennifer Saunders for sexual assault. Eighteen-year-old Saunders was sentenced to six years imprisonment for dressing up as a man and having sex using dildos with two seventeen-year-old women. She could not be charged under the Age of Consent laws as lesbians have no legal age of consent but instead was charged with indecent assault. Her defence that she dressed as a boy at the women's request in order to hide the fact that this was a lesbian relationship from their families was completely ignored. Judge Crabtree, presiding at the trial, scaled new heights of crassness when he said that he supposed that the two young women would rather have been raped by a young man than a woman in disguise.

LABIA (Lesbians Answer Back in Anger) picketed the Lord Chancellor's office to have Crabtree removed from the bench and challenged the lesbian and gay community's seeming silence over the court case. There is some question as to why more lesbians did not become involved in the campaigning around Saunders' case. Cherry Smyth, in her book *Lesbians Talk Queer Notions* asks whether this might be as a result of 'moral disapproval of the dildo or of the ultra-butch', whilst others have argued that it was Saunders' own lawyers who hesitated about her case becoming a *cause célèbre*. The fact remains that Saunders' crime was to dress up as a man to have sex and it is appalling to think that her initial sentence was longer than those frequently handed out to male rapists.[4]

However, although queer politics promoted the notion of lesbians and gay men working together equally under their queer umbrella, lesbians have not always found it easy to co-exist with their queer brothers. Some have pointed out that the formation of lesbian affinity groups such as LABIA within Outrage! shows just how difficult it was for lesbians and gay men to prioritise their issues equally. In 1991, lesbians and gay men from Outrage! and Stonewall called a rally to protest about the imprisonment of a group of gay men for practising consenting SM acts as a result of the notorious Operation Spanner.[5] At the same time, Paragraph 16 of the draft guidance notes to the 1989 Children Act contained the statement that 'Equal Rights' and 'Gay Rights' should have no place in fostering and adoption decisions. This came in a climate where lesbians' access to artificial insemination was being successfully limited through government legislation.[6]

However, there was a tendency amongst some gay men in Outrage! to prioritise Operation Spanner over Paragraph 16 and campaigning about child-care issues was seen as a distinctly lesbian activity – regardless of the fact that there are many gay men out there who wish both to parent and to foster. This is not to negate the importance of campaigning against the trial around Operation Spanner, since the fact that consensual sexual activities can result in imprisonment is appalling and sets a dreadful precedent in British law. One Yorkshire police force later tried to invoke the Spanner precedent when it raided a private party of gay men, totally without justification.

Quim was also rather cynical about what it saw as the new breed of gay man. Or as it put it 'Same old shit, different boys'.

There's a brand of boy around at the moment who reckon that just because you're a pro-sex dyke . . . you have forgotten your feminism and they can get away with sexist put downs, anti-women jokes and all the rest . . . These boys should remember that despite our differences, and the variations in our backgrounds/perspectives, we all have something in common and it begins with a 'W' and doesn't have a dick. (Unless it comes in a toy box and straps on, of course.)[7]

However, the most controversial aspect of Outrage! politics was its preparedness to use outing of closet lesbians and gay men as a political weapon. In 1991 the affinity group FROCS (Faggots Rooting out Closeted Sexuality) threatened to out three lesbian or gay MPs, one from each political party. The story dominated the tabloids and at a hysterical press conference, the FROCS activists announced it was all an elaborate hoax. They had never intended to out anybody – they just wanted to expose tabloid hypocrisy. The best story around at the time was that FROCS only abandoned their outing plan when they were tipped off that the woman MP they wanted to out was not actually a dyke, she was only ugly enough to look like one. In 1995 Outrage! returned to outing in its campaign against closet priests within the Church of England; it outed some priests but also put pressure on some bishops to come out. Again, major media attention followed, but David Hope, soon to be Archbishop of York, spiked the Outrage! guns by deciding it was better to be a grey area than a gay one.

Outing remains a difficult issue for many lesbians and gay men. How much good the outing of closet individuals can ever be for the lesbian and gay whole is open to opinion. The notion that once outed, closet queers will turn in gratitude to their outers is bizarre. No one has convincingly been able to explain just what else outing will achieve, except for increased sales of tabloid newspapers and magazines.

Many lesbians have doubts about both the efficacy and the morality of outing. Lesbians still have a lower status in society than their gay brothers. It is often hard enough to be a woman, let alone a lesbian, in a heterosexist, homophobic society. Whilst there is little doubt that lesbian visibility would be greatly enhanced if a few more influential and successful lesbians came out, there is no point forcing them kicking and screaming out of the closet. Outing works on the principle that lesbian and gay men's experiences, both of the closet and of oppression, are the same. The other big problem with outing is who decides who should and should not be outed. That one group of people, mostly male, feel they can act as judge and jury over other people's lives is no different from the tabloid mentality they are supposed to despise.

As the 1990s have progressed, many lesbians have moved away from Outrage! politics. At the heart of this may lie the continuing clash of personalities that has marked all gay politics, and at the same time Outrage! itself seemed to go through something of a political lull. Also, there has been a belief that somehow lesbians do not really enjoy direct political action. This was politely explained away as being a result of the increased oppression that lesbians face both as women and dykes. The formation in 1994 of the Lesbian Avengers, a direct action group that concentrates solely on lesbian issues, suggests that this old chestnut might be somewhat mistaken. When the comedienne, Sandi Toksvig was outed by a Sunday newspaper, the Save the Children Fund removed her from the line-up of a royal gala. Lesbian Avengers led the campaign of criticism and Save the Children were forced to issue a grovel-ling apology. Other actions have included a lesbian visibility assault on Laura Ashley and other clothes shops and an attack on Channel Four when it edited out a lesbian kiss from an episode of *Brookside*.[8]

Outrage! politics, with their queer energy and sensibility, have changed the way many lesbians regard political activism. At the same time queer, at its best, brings lesbians and gay men together in political, and indeed social, interaction. We have seen how Section 28 and AIDS activism laid the ground for this coming together. Queer politics has also shaken the complacency out of gay politics. After all, there is no place for lesbian and gay apologists in the queer world. Groups like PUSSY and LABIA are distinctly queer because they focus their politics so clearly on our sexuality. Their most successful actions were focused very strongly on promoting lesbian sex-uality, whether it be through the work of Della Grace or in the case against Jennifer Saunders. This is in great contrast to the lesbian feminist approach that is based upon using politics to win the struggle. The Outrage! style is confrontational and lesbians within Outrage! were not afraid to use their sexuality to make that confrontation.

However, the arrival of queer and its appropriation by some talented lesbian artists, writers and photographers, has allowed lesbians to play around with their sexuality like never before. Indeed, the lesbian photographer Della Grace has used gay male imagery in photographs to great, and indeed chal-lenging, effect. Her photograph, 'Lesbian Cock' shows two lesbians clearly parodying their macho leather queen brothers: one brandishes her dildo as if to say 'Here's my cock, now deal with it.' There is a message here for both the gay man who believes he has the monopoly on sex and sexuality, and the lesbian who believes that a dyke in a dildo is no better than a heterosexist man. The image is witty but at the same time challenging and highly sexual. Not all Grace's pictures are as accomplished, but nevertheless Grace has moved from the slightly predictable SM pictures of *Love Bites* to photographs that ask interesting questions of queer sex and sexuality. Other lesbian photographers, too, like Tessa Boffin[9] and Laurence Jaugey-Paget[10] have not only chronicled the growth of queer but also created a new sexual imagery that is direct, empowering and erotic. They have created a visual language that portrays the power of lesbianism through sexual imagery. Grace's pictures, particularly, forever push the boundaries of what is sexually acceptable within a lesbian and gay community.

Queer has also been immensely successful in changing how lesbians, gay men and heterosexuals have approached theatre, art, photography and literature. The arts are the perfect forum for a queer consciousness and sensibility because they actively encourage experimentation and adventure. Queer culture is deeply freeing because it does not need the political baggage that feminist art or literature inevitably brought with it. Lesbian literature has been largely dominated by the life- and lesbian-affirming coming out story which served as much as anything to present us with a blueprint of how to be a happy lesbian. Indeed, in many lesbian romances, lesbianism becomes a glorious universal panacea, helping us to sort out our experiences of breast cancer, child abuse and sexual frigidity. The books of lesbian writers like Sarah Schulman and Jane DeLynn, who have been influenced by a more queer aesthetic, do not present the rosy tinted world of the lesbian romance but a more gritty, honest and sometimes, therefore, more depressing vision of what it is to be a lesbian. Likewise, gay theatre remained in a state of naivety and simplification until Tony Kushner's *Angels in America* blasted gay theatre into the queer 1990s. The plays of the American-born writer Phyllis Nagy seem far more strongly influenced by a queer aesthetic than a lesbian feminist one.[11]

There has been much talk among lesbians of queer sexuality and queer sex. Certainly queer does try to challenge the notions of both a fixed-male and -female sexuality. The natural extension of this is that lesbians and gay men can enjoy sex together under the queer banner. In the past lesbians and gay men have kept rather silent about their occasional toings and froings between each other's bedrooms. These days sex with someone of the opposite gender does not automatically mean expulsion from the lesbian playground. Queer sex bases itself on a real confidence about ourselves and our sexuality and says that we thus do not need to limit our sexual horizons to purely lesbian sex. In some senses this is a strange echo of the lesbian feminist belief that being a lesbian was much more than being about who you go to bed with, though not many lesbian feminists would thank me for saying so. Queer, though, makes a divide between what is your sexual identity and your sexual practice.

Queer sex, then, sounds all very appealing and exciting. The news that we have permission to sleep with our queer brothers if we want to leaves many of us asking 'So what?' Whilst we may now have the confidence to have the sort of sex we want with whoever we want, what does that actually achieve? This is a valid question: one of the weaknesses of queer has been that it only really appeals to other queers. While artists and academics have responded to its possibilities, the majority of people couldn't give a bugger.

Queer has also repossessed such outdated notions as SM and butch/femme. Butch and femme have been stripped of their lesbian identities and been turned into sexual positions, tops and bottoms, subs and doms. SM has been cleansed of its old contentious definitions of violence and abuse. Instead it has been re-modelled as a healthy, sexy alternative to a repressive vanilla sex mentality.

Queer itself relies on the fun of being dangerously transgressive. It forgets that by our very natures, most lesbians and gay men are practised transgressors anyway. It is hard to see just how far our need to transgress will take us. In the summer of 1995, Della Grace announced that she was about to marry her queer brother Jonny Volcano. It would, she assured us, be a truly 'queer wedding'. I hope she takes this new queer transgression to its upmost limit – a Wimpey home in Milton Keynes, perhaps? I am, of course, deliberately missing the queer point. However, the world is hardly watching when Della steps down the aisle. While queer continues to exist mainly as an internal memo to the lesbian and gay community, its true transgressive power is safely limited. It is boring to say, but queer transgression does as little to end lesbian and gay oppression as does living in a lesbian separatist commune.

But just who are the queers transgressing against? Just as lesbian SM was for many lesbians a response to what they saw as the prescriptive sexuality of lesbian feminism, so queer sexuality has followed that tradition. The pro-sex dykes of the late 1980s are the queer lesbians of the 1990s – they have just got a little bit queerer. At the same time, however, this sexiness and this queerness has made lesbianism far more exciting to the straight world than ever before. I do not really believe that lesbian chic is in itself a queer phenomenon, it is more that the presence of queer and the confidence that it brings has allowed lesbians to be just as 'in your face' as their gay brothers.

The 1990s have also seen a growing 'dildo culture' amongst lesbians. In the 1970s and 1980s dildos were considered to be the ultimate in phallocentric possessions. A dyke wielding a dildo would be simply trying, or pretending, to be a man. The dildo in the 1990s may have the same sexual function, but it does not have the same sexual meaning. Contrary to views of lesbian feminists like Sheila Jeffreys, the 1990s dildo is really less of a male penis and more of a female one.

> What is astonishing is the lack of a widespread lesbian revolt against the incursion of the dildo, a symbol of male power and the oppression of women, into lesbian culture. The lesbian pornographers and sex industrialists are telling us that lesbians are disadvantaged by the absence of a penis. They are repeating and promoting all the most oppressive sexological mythmaking.[12]

Actually, many lesbians are now making the best of 'the incursion of the dildo'. And if they are not actually enjoying them, they are certainly buying them. The 'dildo stalls' at Pride continue to do a splendid business and lesbian companies like Belt Up and Buckle Off and Babes continue to do a roaring trade. I do wonder how many of the lesbians who rushed out to buy their beautiful, silicone 'babes', actually use them. It was Della Grace who pointed out the SM dykes' greatest secret was how often she had vanilla sex – the same could be true of dildo owners.

It is also arguable whether or not the fact that lesbians are buying, and presumably enjoying, lesbian-manufactured and marketed sex toys really means they are marching hand in glove with the sexologists. They are, of course, if you believe that lesbian sex exists only as a way of challenging patriarchy. But we have seen again and again how this view of sexuality has become outdated. Neither do I really believe that the sexologists wield the same influence on lesbians now as they did before the 1970s. Whether we like it or not, lesbian politics is continually evolving and it is a sad reality that as we get older it gets much harder to evolve with it. To hint that just because the 1990s lesbian owns a dildo she must be some sort of a political half-wit, under-estimates both her political potential and her political savvy. The 1990s lesbian knows that the best challenge to patriarchy need not necessarily come from the women-only discussion group, it also comes from the streets. The separatism and separation that lie at the heart of a lesbian feminist ethos have been replaced with the notion that lesbians should be among heterosexual society and be out.

Is Jeffreys really right to criticise this new 1990s dildocracy? Some writers have made great claims for the dildo – it doesn't just replace the penis, it actually improves on it. After all, your dildo will never go soft at the crucial moment. Arguments about penetration that were around in the 1970s seem scarcely relevant now. Lesbians do actively seek out and enjoy penetrative sex and this does not seem to make them any less lesbian or any less feminist. Whether you like it or not, to be a feminist in the 1990s is not so much about how you present your politics to the lesbian or feminist caucus than how you can make your feminism work for you in a wider heterosexual context. This is one of the changes that the Thatcher 1980s, with their gradual erosion of the collective ethos, have brought us. In this context, whether you use a dildo or not, or even whether or not you regularly tie your partner up and piss on her, becomes strangely irrelevent.

But what hours of fun we can have speculating on the power of the pseudo-penis. The dildo is much more than some nicely styled silicone. It can represent the lesbian colonisation of male power, or the lesbian's control of her new, burgeoning sexuality. Once the tool of the patriarchy, the penis has become the weapon of a lesbian sexuality that plays patriarchy at its own game. Well that's the theory. We can pretend that the dildo has deeper resonances for our lesbian sexualities, but in the end it's just a piece of silicone. The dildo, like queer politics, is fun to play with. It can make you come but it doesn't really make you think. In the narrow arena of the lesbian bedroom, a dildo may have profound political resonance, but in the wider world it is just a sex toy.

There is no doubt that politics in Britain in the 1990s have largely re-privatised sex. It is interesting to see how queer, rather than challenging this privatisation, has actually played subtly into it. This is because queer pitches its politics squarely at our life-styles rather than our ideologies. The queer politics of organisations like Outrage! do not meld into our daily lives in the same way as lesbian feminism tried to blend politics and life-style and life-style and politics.

Jeffreys and other writers who criticise the politics of queer do strike a chord when they talk of the de-politicising of the lesbian movement in the 1990s. This does not mean that lesbians will not be able to respond to political challenges: it suggests that lesbian politics, lacking any basic ideologies, have become re-active rather than pro-active. In the 1970s and 1980s, the media ignored lesbians because they were so intensely dreary and political – it is no coincidence that the media now loves the lesbian because she is so exciting but so intensely non-political. The chic lesbian is interesting to a male-based media because she is far more untransgressive than her lesbian feminist foremothers. Lesbians' concern about the current media obsession with lesbian chic is based on the real perception that fashions change. Whilst lesbianism has never had such a high profile, featuring in three out of the four major soap operas, we are all aware of how quickly lesbians will slip from the heterosexual consciousness.

It would be nice to think that the current wave of articles about lesbianism (which have been appearing for well over a year now) might perhaps even show lesbianism in a favourable light. As recent features in London's *Time Out*[13] and the *Sunday Times*[14] suggest, lesbians may now come in fancy clothes but they are still treated with the same amount of ridicule and contempt that they have always been. Yet the lesbian and gay scene seems to suggest that there are more and more young lesbians out there (though this may just be my own perception as I struggle into my thirties). Indeed, the Albert Kennedy Trust, which provides support for lesbians and gay men who have become homeless because of their sexuality, reports an increase in the number of younger lesbians turning to them for help. This is, perhaps, the other side of the Beth Jordache story – homophobia is much more real than the soap operas would have us believe and being lesbian or gay is not always about being fashionable.

Lesbian chic also relies heavily on the new lesbian commercialism. The chic lesbian is totally dependent on the latest fashionable garment and the latest fashionable place to be seen. Lesbians can really only buy into the lesbian chic machine if they have the looks, the figures and the bank balances to carry it all off. Lesbian and gay clubs have become distinctly fashion-conscious, encouraging a much younger and trendier crowd. This leaves many older lesbians out on a lesbian limb. It is no coincidence that some lesbians in Todmorden, West Yorkshire have stopped going to their monthly women-only disco because it has become over-run by lesbians from Manchester and beyond. There is no longer any space within their own cities where they feel comfortable partying.

The problem with much of this new lesbian commercialism is that it is rarely controlled by lesbians themselves. Thus clubs and pubs and cafes are dependent on gay men's patronage to ensure their survival. Not only this, but the gay male control of many of our social spaces means that lesbians often have to fit in with gay male ideas of what makes a good bar or a decent club.

The gradual moving together of lesbians and gay men, whether socially or politically, has been of much concern to those remaining lesbian feminist writers. They believe that gay men are fundamentally hostile to lesbian rights. They are also deeply concerned by the continued lesbian mimicking of gay male style and politics. The queer lesbian in the 1990s is almost certainly aware of the shortcomings of her queer brother: just like the *Quim* girls before her, she probably had to challenge their sexism and their assumptions. But the success of Lesbian Avengers suggests that lesbians may well be able to take good care of themselves.

The politics of the Lesbian Avengers are intrinsically re-active. They, like other forms of 'in your face' activism rely on a symbiotic relationship between the TV camera and the activist. But the relationship is not actually an equal one and it will be interesting to see just how extreme Lesbian Avenger actions will have to become to keep the Avengers on the British media's mailing list. One Avenger action in 1995 was in response to what they considered a racist book review by a lesbian journalist. Regardless of whether the article was racist or not, it is of some concern when lesbians start policing other lesbians. The best thing about queer politics and the activism of the Lesbian Avengers is that they confront heterosexuality and heterosexual attitudes. Their power will be lost if they turn their gaze inward. Lesbian feminism, on the other hand, was never reliant on media, or indeed commercial agendas. It relied on a series of networks whose roots could be found deep within the Women's Liberation Movement. We can see how these networks have been eroded from both within and without the movement and it is easy to see why many women have become not only disenchanted by, but also disenfranchised from, current lesbian politics. Lesbianism in the 1990s seems to be continually buffeted between the twin pressures of other people's commercialism and other people's political agendas. Lesbian feminism in the early 1980s gave us the platform to discuss what we wanted and how we wanted it, the great tragedy being, of course, that when we had this women-centred opportunity we blew it. It is surprising that we have replaced a single ideology which we were all supposed to agree with or else, with no ideology at all.

However, there have also been some positive advances. The last three years have also seen a new energy in specifically lesbian film-making. The 1994 hit film *Go Fish*[15] was a sassy, witty and imaginative slice of lesbian life. 1995 saw the successful release of the delightful lesbian skating romance *Blue Ice*,[16] and in the same year the video company Dangerous to Know produced the very funny lesbian spoof *M.u.f.f Match*. All these films were produced for lesbians by lesbians, but at the same time find a much wider audience. In these films, lesbianism is not presented as the 'issue' or the 'problem', nor is the sexuality of the protagonists some nifty plot device.

Queer has also excited a whole generation of academics. Whilst Women's Studies is generally derided as being too unbelievably pc, lesbian and gay studies in their new queer packaging have never been more trendy. Queer studies have spawned a new lesbian and gay language. With just the briefest reading of a bit of Michel Foucault, we can now enjoy our 'binary discourses' and our 'polymorphous perversities'; we can even have a construct here and a hegemony there. But unlike the feminist movement of the 1970s and the 1980s, queer is a movement that has no real meat. It sets us up in opposition to existing mores, both heterosexual and homosexual, but it never suggests what that opposition will achieve. It glories in transgression but never suggests where that transgression will lead us. It allows endless speculation and endless theorising because it never offers us conclusions. Thus, queer becomes ideal as an academic exercise, a dog forever chasing a increasingly scruffy tail.

Queer politics, sexuality and arts have dominated the lesbian 1990s, but they have also left many lesbians in something of a political quandary. Those lesbians who bravely continue to champion lesbian feminist ideals remain as criticised and ridiculed as they were in the late 1980s. There is no doubt that the world has changed around them and their politics have not kept time with these changes, but they do deserve some recognition for their achievements. The rise of queer has depoliticised lesbianism to the point that our sexuality becomes little more than a life-style choice, easily commodified and commercialised. Lesbian chic has brought a new kudos to being a dyke in the 1990s, but it brings with it no politics or no real lesbian power. It is a bimbo culture.

Whilst the successful actions of the Lesbian Avengers show that there is still a lesbian political spirit out there, the growing commercialism of the lesbian and gay scene, with its emphasis on fashion rather than politics, is again in danger of encouraging us to turn our gaze upon ourselves. This new lesbian and gay complacency could be both dangerous and narrowsighted. In the meantime, we can always polish up our dildos. I am sure that together we can find some new and terrifically exciting ways to be transgressive. The question is: will anybody notice?

On The Cutting Edge Of Something . . .

Towards a lesbian millennium

Wander down Old Compton Street in London and the streets around and you will think you're in a different world. Gay cafes, gay shops and gay bars abound. Nowhere is the commercialism of the gay scene more apparent or more vibrant. In Manchester, Edinburgh, even Blackpool, smaller 'gay villages' are thriving, where once we had 'gay ghettos'. Yet there is a danger that as we approach the new millennium we will turn the lesbian and gay community into nothing more than a sophisticated playground. Lesbian and gay politics have been reduced to two political factions, one obsessed with column inches, the other obsessed with growing bank balances. We have lost that collective energy that aimed at major political change and have become obsessed instead with single-issue politics. Lesbian politics, which twenty years ago were beginning to have an identity all their own, are being subsumed in a post-queer, homosexual whole.

The lesbian sex wars of the 1980s challenged our notions of a single lesbian body politic. The anger that sexual practices like SM and butch/femme role-playing engendered was often out of all proportion to the numbers of lesbians who were actually doing them. The very existence of a number of sexual practices that some lesbians found unacceptable was enough to create lesbian sex wars. As the 1980s progressed, the sex radical faction began to get an upper hand. Those who opposed SM, once a dominating voice in lesbian politics, became more silent as the trappings of a more exciting sexual practice caught the lesbian imagination. Lesbian sex wars, arguments about what is and is not lesbian sexuality, have made us wary of trying to create a new lesbian ideology. We do not want, nor do we really have the economic or practical resources, to go back to a time when everything about us had to be analysed, questioned or judged by the lesbian collective.

In the mid-1990s, feminism has become a dirty word, both in a wider society and in our own community. We are now creating our own lesbian backlash. Political correctness, once used to protect and enshrine lesbian and gay rights, is now being used to attack them. But we forget that a right-wing Tory MP's pc is what we would consider a basic human right. In the 1990s we too have become obsessed with rooting out the pc amongst us. Old values that promulgate women-only spaces, waged or unwaged entry fees, easy disabled access, become too easily labelled politically correct. Yes, there were lesbian feminist pc excesses, like the wombyn and the wimmin, but these should not be used to denigrate the whole. And nor should anyone who dares to criticise the post-queer status quo become a target of the new anti-pc police. The idea that we must put our politics and consciences in cold storage while we all go out and party could be dangerously short-sighted. But it is too damn pc to be political.

And political correctness plays into our need to be transgressive. We always need to have something to transgress against. The worst result of the lesbian sex wars has been our creation of the lesbian 'Nanny' figure. Much of the lesbian imagery we create for ourselves in the 1990s is dependent on the shadowy figure we have plucked from the 1970s and early 1980s. 'Nanny' stops us having our 1990s sexy, queer fun, it is she who tells us that we can't have our lesbian cake and eat her too. It is 'Nanny' who stops us wearing our dildos and 'Nanny' who we are criticising when we write off lesbian feminist opinion. But the lesbian feminist 'Nanny' figure really doesn't exist. She might have done in the 1970s, she might have done in the early 1980s, but now she has been silenced and is generally silent herself. Yet we seem to be trapped in the idea that we must forever show her just how naughty we can be. We seem to be convinced that we can only ever shock ourselves into discovering our lesbian capabilities.

The spring and summer of 1995 saw the arrival of the latest manifestation of the modern lesbian when the new fashion for drag kings came to London. Drag kingery is cross-dressing for dykes and is currently at the cutting edge of lesbian fashion, championed by the ubiquitous Della Grace. The opening of Club Knave in London brought drag kings out in all their finery, as lesbians donned their cloth caps and glued on their moustaches, dressing up as construction workers, policemen etc. (all very Village People). Needless to say, drag kings originally came from America (one day British lesbian and gay men will do something truly original and transgressive before their American cousins). Sheila Jeffreys has not yet written about this new lesbian phenomenon, but you can bet your bottom dollar that she will. Lesbians have spent the last thirty years trying to show the heterosexual world that we are not trying to be pseudo-men, and suddenly we are. Those who have criticised the gradual sublimation of lesbian identities within gay male homosexuality will find this latest manifestation of the lesbian both silly and depressing.

Drag queens, gay men who parody women, have long stood as the totems of the lesbian and gay movement. It was they who instigated the Stonewall Riot and the birth of gay politics as we know it. The new drag king thing seems a sad mimicking of gay male culture, a bizarre twist on penis envy. More depressingly still, there will be a wave of queer and post-queer writing that will tell us how deeply progressive all this is. We will be told that drag kings are not mimicking gay men, but 'borrowing' (the trendy post-queer buzzword) from gay male cultures and notions of heterosexual masculinity. We will, no doubt, be told that drag kings subvert ideas of femininity and change our perceptions of our lesbian sexuality. These bearded wonders will be presented not as symbolic of the paucity of lesbian ideas but as part of our new lesbian sophistication.

But there is also something rather cheering in the idea that lesbians are now so confident in their sexuality that they can start to play around with it and even parody it. In the 1970s, lesbians fought to find that confidence which we now take so much or granted. Lesbian feminism, which has become defined by many as a highly prescriptive movement, actually allowed women to explore and come to terms with their own lesbian sexuality. Lesbianism gained both a political importance and a political imperative through it. But in the search to find a valid definition of lesbian sexuality, certain lesbian feminists did seem to impose too many rules and regulations. A movement that sought to change society seemed to become obsessed with only changing itself, and those who wanted to talk about new ideas and new challenges often felt marginalised and silenced.

In the 1990s, there is no monolithic lesbian sexuality, there are lesbian sexualities. This is the lesson of the lesbian sex wars, but it is a lesson we have only part understood. We have actually succeeded in creating a lesbian world where we can enjoy a plurality of styles, views and sexual behaviours. We can define our lesbian sexualities how we want, or choose not to define them at all. But you wouldn't always know it.

There is a danger that our media only represents one image of the 1990s lesbian. She is invariably the sexiest and the most fashionable. She wears the right clothes and goes to the right places. She has to be seen to be sexual and sexually aware. She always has to be on the cutting edge of something. More importantly, those lesbians who do not meet the current lesbian trends are largely silenced. Rather than portray the multi-faceted nature of our lesbian community, we focus on the lesbian images and issues that make us most comfortable and ask fewest questions. Whilst it is alright to be 'radically queer', it is all wrong to be 'political'. 'Political' conjures up images of hairy-legged lesbianism with its hang-ups about sexuality and its dreary, serious intentions. I am not advocating a return to lesbian feminist values. Lesbian feminism has lost its place in our consciousnesses for many different, complicated reasons. The lesbian sex wars showed that it could be rigid, inflexible to new ideas and far from all-embracing. I am just concerned that we are close to creating a notion of lesbianism that is just as rigid and inflexible. I do not welcome a new lesbian millennium where we must all look the same, think the same and do the same. Our ideas of what makes a decent 1990s lesbian, that she has an up-front sexuality, that she uses

sex toys, that she champions fashion could be just as proscriptive as the lesbians of the 1980s who railed against frilly
knickers.

The 1990s have brought, I believe, a real Londonisation to
our politics. The lesbian and gay media is now virtually controlled from London, and London phenomena (including drag
kings and even Lesbian Avengers) often dominate our perception of current lesbian, and indeed gay, male culture. Many of
the lesbian sex wars were fought in London, many of the
events discussed in previous chapters of this book took place in
London, but these took place alongside lesbian networks that
often spread nationwide. As economics have changed, and our
lives have changed with them, many of these networks have
been eroded. We are now left with newspapers and magazines
and even television and radio that peddle a London-based
agenda. It is unfashionable to say it, but not all lesbians and
gay men enjoy the cappuccino culture that Old Compton
Street represents.

Perhaps it is just that we are losing sight of what it really
means to be radical. It was a radical act to make a space for
ourselves in a hostile, heterosexual world. So, it is important
that we have built cafes and bars right in the heart of central
London, but to then sit in those bars and drink our coffee and
our continental lagers is maybe not so radical after all. As we
approach the next millennium, complacency should not be
part of our political agenda.

We should not devalue the contribution of a lesbian magazine like *Diva* or the producers of *Dyke TV* to our new lesbian
life-style. But we should point out that there is a large lesbian
community out there that is not always represented by our
glossy magazines or the latest post-queer publication. You

might be forgiven for assuming, for example, that lesbian feminism has now totally been discarded and that writers and academics like Sheila Jeffreys are just voices in the lesbian wilderness. True, the lesbian feminist voice has been largely silenced, but the lesbian feminists are still here. Lesbians valiantly struggle to produce the lesbian feminist magazine, *Trouble and Strife*, and their fundamental concerns about SM and other sexual practices have not been totally abandoned.

We are often our own harshest critics, much keener to attack each other or to judge each other than to defend. During the lesbian sex wars we saw how again and again we personalised our disputes, blaming individuals rather than ideas and ideologies. Today, it doesn't take too long for lesbians in the spotlight to become ridiculed or attacked. We have trained ourselves to have the lowest boredom threshold where our lesbian heroines are concerned. Even such a practised transgressor as Della Grace is suffering from our collective 'Della fatigue'. We seem to find it much easier to concentrate our energies on eulogising the pretend lesbians amongst us. Beth Jordache, *Brookside*'s erstwhile heroine, is really nothing more than a ratings-war creation – but how much we have invested in that character's success. She is the brave lesbian fighting homophobia, fighting violence and sexual abuse. She is the brave lesbian holding firm to her femme roots. Oh, what a load of rubbish! She is the pseudo-lesbian, created as much for the male viewer as the lesbian. She is a collection of issues masquerading as a fully-rounded character. And when the lesbianism becomes less interesting, then she's slaughtered in the stroke of a pen.

The lesbian and gay playground we have created with its 'anything goes as long as its transgressive' energy could be just as much a closet as the underground world of clubs and bars we habited before our gay liberation. The media's obsession with lesbian chic just tells us how they can treat us like so many fleas in a travelling flea circus. We perform our tricks and briefly the straight world applauds. Many lesbians have been critical of lesbian chic, they have seen how it focuses upon the acceptable and the non-threatening among us. They comment on how it has created an image of the heterosexualised lesbian, a non-political, good-time girl. Yet *we* have bought that image too. Whilst we are desperate to transgress amongst ourselves, we seem only too pleased to fall into the straight media's ideas of who should and shouldn't be a lesbian.

Lesbian sex continually provides us with the best way to be transgressive. Sex makes us different, and it is this difference that becomes such a powerful lesbian weapon. Lesbian feminism used that power to find a sort of lesbian autonomy. In the 1990s we seem to be searching for a sexuality that is both exclusive and inclusive. It is almost like if we lose the media's attention then we lose the point of being lesbian at all.

Some lesbians criticise the growing together of the lesbian and gay male scene. I came out in mixed lesbian and gay communities, we did not have the energy or the economic independence to create a regular women-only scene. I have always enjoyed working with gay men and playing with gay men. But that does not mean that I want to fuck them or I think that somehow our two sexualities are the same. Queer has tried to suggest that old notions of lesbian and gay identities can be lost under the banner of 'polymorphous perversity', I do not believe this can or should be done. Lesbians, in the early 1990s, were all too aware of the difficulties of working in a mixed lesbian, gay or queer dynamic. They were, and still are, aware that gay men do not necessarily share an understanding of what it is to be a lesbian.

In the autumn of 1995, scientific research seemed to suggest that gay men at least were born, not made. Studies suggested that there were differences in the X chromosome between gay men and their heterosexual brothers. But the same sorts of patterns could not be found in lesbians. If all this research is discovered to be true, then where does that leave lesbians and gay men? The new queer and post-queer lesbian and gay alliances may seem a little fragile in these circumstances if no scientific cause for lesbianism is discovered. Lesbians have always had to champion their own sexuality in mixed gay groupings in a way that gay men have never had to do. It will be interesting to see what value is placed on new gay theories if the root cause of homosexuality has really been discovered. Lesbians have largely won their fight to be included in the gay male consciousness. In the 1990s, this has often been the result of playing gay men's games. In 1993, some lesbians even tried to cruise on Hampstead Heath, the regular gay men's cruising ground. To be continually aping gay men's sexuality, seeking gay men's approval and validation, does not seem what we went through feminism or the lesbian sex wars for. New scientific study might yet make such games redundant, but lesbians may once again have to find strategies to combat this 1990s-style 'sexology'.

More to the point perhaps, these studies lead us to consider once again how very little we know of our own sexuality. Lesbian feminist ideology defined lesbianism as a positive, political choice, socially constructed. Other lesbians challenged these ideas, feeling their sexuality came from somewhere very different, suggesting they were born that way.

In the 1990s, lesbianism often seems to be something we might call a 'life-style choice', just as socially constructed as the lesbian feminist model but without the complicated, 'anti-sex' politics. Just as we scarcely understand the meanings of butch and femme within our own history and our psyches, so it may prove to be with our lesbian sexuality.

The point then is to live our lesbianism as best we can. As we move towards the millennium, we should be aware that though we can play in relative freedom, there may be less easy times ahead. There seems to be highly insidious, but definitely growing, right-wing extremism building in our country. Mixed into this right-wing message is the re-emergence of the dreaded 'family values'. Single mothers have become an easy target because they have no economic clout, but there is no reason to suppose that lesbians and gay men won't soon face some attack. The lesbian and gay response has been largely to sit with our fingers crossed and wait for the arrival of a Labour government. But New Labour seems to be lurching right itself. I believe that the protection of the family will become even more of a political weapon and that attacks on lesbian and gay rights within this will be more oblique, but probably more effective. Our rights to have access to our children or to have children ourselves may come under attack. For there is no reason to suppose that just as we have become more effective at challenging homophobia, so the homophobes won't have learnt to be more efficiently homophobic.

It is not enough, I believe, to leave all our politics up to the Stonewall Group and all our displays of angry homosexuality to Outrage! or to Lesbian Avengers. In our efforts to escape the grim realities of the lesbian sex wars, we have allowed our politics to become buried in our search for lesbian pleasure. This strategy has brought us into the heterosexual spotlight. I do not disagree that it has become easier to be out and to be a lesbian or that lesbianism is more acceptable than it hitherto has been. But, in 1996, it is not just political correctness that has faced harsh criticism, the whole of liberal politics is being placed under the spotlight. That is how the Right are using the politics of the family. There is now a distinct danger that our greatest allies will themselves feel the sting of the approaching backlash.

As we approach the new millennium, let us at least recognise how much we have achieved. At the beginning of this century, lesbianism was, at best, a sickness and, at worst, active degeneracy. Lesbian sex may not have been criminalised as were homosexual sexual acts, but lesbians themselves were just as hated, feared and ridiculed. In the 1950s and 1960s lesbians seemed to exist in a shadowy, underground world, sometimes mimicking heterosexual society, but never a part of it. In the 1970s, the Gay Liberation Front and Women's Liberation changed the status of the lesbian forever. Our growing cohesion as an effective political body has brought our existence into the hearts and minds of heterosexual society. We can still be ridiculed, but somehow the ridicule seems more hollow. Our confidence and our style make us a force to be reckoned with.

But if the twentieth century has been the century of the homosexual, then we have a way to go before we make the twenty-first the century of the lesbian. We have become so used to the idea that we must forever be outside society that we do not believe that we can ever find a place within its politics. The search for full equality is often linked with the danger of assimilating into the heterosexual world. The simple truth is that gay men and lesbians will never assimilate fully into straight society. We will never lose our 'outsider status' and we will always be 'other'. Those who fear assimilation, of becoming just like our heterosexual peers, forget that as lesbians and gay men we assimilate all the time, in our families, in our workplaces, but heterosexual society will never allow that assimilation to be based on anything other than pretence. In the meantime, we should realise that a politics cannot be a politics until it hits the mainstream. It is only when lesbians find a way into mainstream political theory that our millennium will have arrived. But the cost of this need not be assimilation.

We must also come to terms with the fact that we are all different. The lesbian sex wars were fuelled in part by our fear of diversity and difference. We cannot again create a siege mentality around our sexuality. We must not despise those of us who are not sexual nor those of us who are. Our lesbian credibility must be based on who we are, not what we do in bed. We must try and find an identity for ourselves that stretches a little further than our bedroom. Lesbian chic has created an image of the lesbian that is as unchallenging as it is palatable.

The chic lesbian is a phase that society feels we're going through. And it is a phase we will soon be getting over. Our task must be to make society understand that behind the chic lesbian is another, and another. At the heart of our lesbian politics must be the understanding that our sexuality is the key to who we are. We cannot again choose to subsume our sexual practice in an awkward, unworkable politics. We cannot pretend that being a lesbian need not necessarily involve having sex with women. But neither must we believe that being sexual is all it takes to change the world. Our politics must stretch further than the politics of our own community. They must stretch further than playing around with notions of masculinity, femininity and gender identity. Whilst we frolic in our lesbian and gay playgrounds, we can sometimes influence politics but never change them fundamentally.

It is still true that it is our sexual choice that gives us sexual power. Women are still not supposed to wield the same sexual power as men; we are still expected to be the choice and not the chooser. But part of our sexual power lies in the fact that we come in all shapes and sizes, with different backgrounds and experiences. For when we propagate an image of the lesbian as little different than her heterosexual sister, or as a sexy fashion victim on her way to the rave, we short-change ourselves and our history. Our power is much greater than our power to titillate either ourselves or heterosexual males.

On its own, our sexual power is not enough. It can win us many column inches, it can bring us trendiness and temporary glamour. But we must not allow this temporary glamour to be translated into a passing phase. Having made the gains we have made, we must not wallow in the media's shadow. We must quit the search for new and more glamorous or daring ways to be a lesbian. We do not need to be forever playing with our genders or our identities: I think we know who we are. For until we find a new lesbian politics which embraces all our histories and all our identities, we can never create our lesbian millennium. It is nice to create a lesbian playground where we can have the sort of sex we want, when we want it. But to be on the cutting edge of something isn't quite enough.

Notes

Essential Sex

1. Lillian Faderman, *Surpassing the Love of Men* (The Women's Press 1980).
2. Jeffrey Weeks, *Sexuality and its Discontents* (Routledge 1985).
3. Radclyffe Hall, *The Well of Loneliness* (Virago 1982, first published 1928).
4. Lillian Faderman's book *Surpassing the Love of Men* remains the key text for discussing 'romantic friendships' among women. For contemporary reactions to the publishing of the *The Well*, see Part 3, Chapter 2.
5. S. Freud, *The Psychogenesis of a Case of Homosexuality in Women*, quoted in Faderman pp. 323–24.
6. Maureen Duffy, *The Microcosm* (Virago 1990, first published by Hutchinson 1966).
7. Ann Bannon, *I am a Woman* (Naiad Press 1986, first published 1959), pp. 85–6.
8. From *Come Together*, the newsletter of GLF, 1971.
9. Sheila Jeffreys, *The Lesbian Heresy* (Women's Press 1994), p. vii.

10. Adrienne Rich, *Compulsory Heterosexuality and Lesbian Existence* (Onlywomen Press 1982).

11. Leeds Revolutionary Feminist Group in Lilian Mohin (ed.), *Love Your Enemy? The Debate between Heterosexual Feminism and Political Lesbianism* (Onlywoman Press 1982), p. 5.

12. Sheila Jeffreys, 'Butch and Femme: Now and Then', in Lesbian History Group (eds,) *Not a Passing Phase* (The Women's Press 1989), p. 186.

13. Ruth Everard, 'Talking Dirty', in Emma Healey and Angela Mason (eds), *Stonewall 25* (Virago 1994), p. 251.

14. Celia Kitzinger, *The Social Construction of Lesbianism* (Sage 1987), p. 34.

15. Della Grace, quoted in Cherry Smyth, *Lesbians Talk Queer Notions* (Scarlet Press 1992).

16. Lynne Segal, *Straight Sex: The Politics of Pleasure* (Virago 1994), p. xi.

17. Elizabeth Wilson, 'I'll Climb The Stairway to Heaven', in Sue Cartledge and Joanne Ryan (eds), *Sex and Love* (Women's Press 1983), p. 194.

Before We Knew Any Better

1. Christa D'Souza, 'Sisters under the Skin', in *The Sunday Times*, 12 March 1995.

2. Richard von Krafft-Ebing, 'Psychopathia Sexualis', quoted in Mandy Merck, 'Transforming the Suit', in Tessa Boffin and J. Fraser (eds), *Stolen Glances* (Pandora Press 1991), p. 24.

3. Diana Chapman, interviewed in Lesbian Oral History

Group, *Inventing Ourselves: Lesbian Life Stories,* Hall Carpenter Archives (Routledge 1989), p. 49.

4. Elizabeth Wilson, 'Making an Appearance', in Tessa Boffin and J. Fraser (eds), *Stolen Glances* (Pandora Press 1991), p. 56.

5. Sheila Jeffreys, 'Butch and Femme: Now and Then', in London History Group (eds), *Not a Passing Phase* (The Women's Press 1989), p. 169.

6. Celia Kitzinger, *The Social Construction of Lesbianism* (Sage 1987), p. 146.

7. Letter from J.B., *Arena 3*, vol. 7, 1970.

8. Letter in *Arena 3*, vol. 8, no. 2, 1971.

9. Letter in *Arena 3*, vol. 8, no. 6, 1971.

10. Letter in *Come Together*, the magazine of GLF, 1971.

11. *Sappho* magazine, vol. 4/3, 1975.

12. Lillian Faderman, *Surpassing the Love of Men* (The Women's Press 1985).

13. For a further discussion of butch/femme, read Esther Newton's essay 'The Mythic Mannish Lesbian', in M. Duberman, M. Vicinus and G. Chancey (eds), *Hidden from History: Reclaiming the Gay and Lesbian Past* (Penguin 1990).

14. Elizabeth Wilson, 'Making an Appearance', in E. Healey and A. Mason (eds), *Stonewall 25* (Virago 1994).

15. Shelia Jeffreys, ibid.

16. Anna Livia, 'I would Rather be Dead than Gone Forever: Butch and Femme as Responses to Patriarchy', in *Gossip*, no. 5, 1988.

17. Joan Nestle, 'The Fem Question', in Carole S. Vance (ed.), *Pleasure and Danger* (Routledge, Kegan Paul 1984), p. 232.

18. Celia Kitzinger, *The Social Construction of Lesbianism* (Sage 1987).

Knowing What's Good For Us

1. Janet Dixon, 'Separatism: a look back in Anger', in Bob Cant and Susan Hemmings (eds), *Radical Records* (Routledge 1988), p. 72.
2. Lilian Mohin (ed.), *Political Lesbianism: The Case Against Heterosexuality* (Onlywomen Press 1981), p. 5.
3. Adrienne Rich, 'Compulsory Heterosexuality and Lesbian Existence' (Onlywomen Press 1984).
4. Mary Daly, *Gyn/Ecology* (The Women's Press 1979).
5. Mary Daly, *Pure Lust* (The Women's Press 1982).
6. Sheila Jeffreys, *The Lesbian Heresy* (Women's Press 1994), p. 1.
7. Wendy Clark, 'The Dyke, The Feminist and The Devil', in *Feminist Review*, 11, Summer 1982, p. 33.
8. ibid.
9. Celia Kitzinger, *Case Studies from The Social Construction of Lesbianism* (Sage 1987), p. 115.
10. Carolle S. Berry and Carol Jones, 'Feminism or Sadomasochism?', in *Revolutionary and Radical Feminist Newsletter*, Autumn 1982.

Pain Without Gain

1. Amber Hollingbaugh and Cherrie Moraga, 'What We're Rollin Around in Bed With. Sexual Silences in Feminism:

A Conversation toward Ending Them' in *Heresies*' 'Sex Issue', 1981.

2. Sheila Jeffreys, 'Butch and Femme: Now and Then', in Lesbian History Group (eds), *Not a Passing Phase* (The Women's Press 1989), p. 189.

3. Carole S. Vance (ed.) *Pleasure and Danger* (Routledge, Kegan Paul 1984), p. xvi.

4. Susan Ardill and Sue O'Sullivan, 'Upsetting an Applecart: Difference, Desire and Lesbian Sadomasochism', in *Feminist Review,* Summer 1986.

5. Pat Califia, 'Feminism and Sadomasochism' in *Heresies*' 'Sex Issue', 1981.

6. Pat Califia, *Macho Sluts* (Alyson 1988).

7. Samois Collective (eds), *Coming to Power: Writings and Graphics on Lesbian S/M* (Alyson 1981).

8. Sue Golding, 'A Walk in the Wild Side', in *London Lesbian Newsletter,* 1982.

9. From *Revolutionary and Radical Feminist Newsletter,* Autumn 1982.

10. For a vivid account of the events at the London Lesbian and Gay Centre read Sue O'Sullivan and Susan Ardill's article 'Upsetting an Applecart'.

11. Sheila Jeffreys, *The Lesbian Heresy* (The Women's Press 1994), p. 99.

12. Sheila Jeffreys, 'Sadomasochism: The Erotic Cult of Fascism', in her *The Lesbian Heresy* (The Women's Press 1994), p. 229.

13. ibid., p. 226.

14. Caroline Claxton, 'Sado-Masochism (Eek!) Stirs Up a Bucketful of Emotions', in *Radical Revolutionary Newsletter*, 1985.

15. Elizabeth Carola, *Spare Rib*, September 1986.
16. Susanna Radecki, *Spare Rib*, September 1986.
17. Paula Jennings, *The Hunt Saboteur in Fox Furs*, Gossip 6 (Onlywomen Press).
18. Julie Bindel, 'Coming to Power, Coming to Britain?', *Revolutionary and Radical Newsletter*, Autumn 1982.

Breaking Down The Barriers

1. Sheila Mclaughlin 1987.
2. Donna Deitch 1985.
3. John Sayles 1983.
4. From *The Lesbian Information Newsletter*, August 1988.
5. Sheila Mclauglin, interviewed in *Screen*, vol. 28, no. 4, Autumn 1987.
6. Joan Nestle, *A Restricted Country* (Sheba Feminist Press 1988).
7. ibid., p. 105.
8. ibid., p. 105.
9. ibid., p. 9.
10. Sheila Jeffreys, 'Butch Femme: Now and Then', in *Not a Passing Phase: Reclaiming Lesbians in History* (The Women's Press 1989).
11. Audre Lorde, *Zami: A New Spelling of my Name* (Pandora 1996, first published Persephone Press 1982), p. 185.
12. Later published as E. Kennedy and M. Davis, *Boots of Leather, Slippers of Gold* (Penguin 1994).
13. *Making Out: The Book of Lesbian Sex and Sexuality*, text by Z. Schramm-Evans, photographs by Laurence Jaugey-Paget (Pandora Press 1995).
14. Catherine Treasure, *Pink Paper* 8, September 1988.

15. For a fuller account of the lesbian summer of love see Susan Ardil and Sue O'Sullivan's article 'The Lesbian Summer of Love', in *Feminist Review,* Autumn 1988.

Getting Wet

1. Sheila Jeffreys, *The Lesbian Heresy* (The Women's Press 1994), p. 35.
2. Sheba Collective (eds), *Serious Pleasure* (Sheba Feminist Publishers 1989).
3. Sheba Collective (eds), Introduction to *Serious Pleasure*.
4. Sue O'Sullivan and Susan Ardill 'Upsetting an Applecart', in *Feminist Review,* Summer 1986.
5. Sue O'Sullivan and Susan Ardill, 'The Lesbian Summer of Love', in *Feminist Review,* Autumn 1988.
6. Barbara Smith, 'The Art of Poise', in Sheba Collective (eds), *Serious Pleasure*, p. 64.
7. Katherine V. Forrest, *Daughters of a Coral Dawn* (Naiad 1984), pp. 208–209.
8. Jewelle Gomez, 'Water with the Wine', in *Serious Pleasure*.
9. Tee Corinne, *Yantras Of Womanlove* (Naiad 1982).
10. Sheila Jeffreys, *The Lesbian Heresy* (The Women's Press 1994), p. 30.
11. *Quim* magazine was published sporadically until 1995.
12. For a flavour of the style and writings of Susie Bright read *Susie Bright's Sexual Reality* (Cleis Press 1992) and *Susie Sexpert's Lesbian Sex World* (Cleis Press 1990).
13. See Jill Posener, *Spray it Loud* (GMP 1982).
14. Editorial, *Quim*, Issue 2, Summer 1991.

15. ibid.
16. Sophie Moorcock, 'Drawing the Invisible Line', in *Quim*, Issue 2, Summer 1991.
17. Sheila Jeffrey, 'Sadomasochism: The Erotic Cult of Fascism', in her *The Lesbian Heresy* (The Women's Press 1994), p. 222.
18. Trash White, 'The Fantasy Debate', in *Quim*, Issue 2, Summer 1991.
19. Sophie Moorcock, 'Drawing the Invisible Line', in *Quim*, Issue 2, Summer 1991.
20. Pat Califia, Introduction to *Macho Sluts* (Alyson 1988).
21. ibid., p. 14.
22. Introduction to Lady Winston (ed.), *The Leading Edge* (Naiad 1988).
23. Sarah Schulman, *After Delores* (Sheba Feminist Publishers 1989), and *People in Trouble* (Sheba Feminist Publishers 1991).
24. Jane Delynn, *Don Juan in the Village* (Serpent's Tail 1991).
25. Sarah Schulman, *People in Trouble* (Sheba Feminist Publishers 1991), p. 180.

Outside Influences

1. Sue O'Sullivan and Pratibher Parmer (eds), *Lesbians Talk Safer Sex* (Scarlet Press 1992), p. 20.
2. Pat Califia, *Sapphistry* (Naiad, first published 1980).
3. *Joy of Lesbian Sex*.
4. JoAnn Loulan, *Lesbian Sex* (Spinsters 1984).
5. JoAnn Loulan, *Lesbian Passion* (Spinsters 1987).
6. *Making Out: The Book of Lesbian Sex and Sexualiy*, text

by Zoe Schramm-Evans, photographs by Laurence Jaugey-Paget (Pandora 1995).
7. ibid., p. 136.

Of Quims And Queers

1. Madonna, *Sex* (Secker and Warburg 1991).
2. For a fuller description of PUSSY, the Outrage! affinity group see Anne Marie Smith, 'Outlaws as Legislators', in V. Harwood, D. Oswell, K. Parkinson and A. Ward (eds), *Pleasure Principles* (Laurence and Wishart 1993).
3. Della Grace, *Love Bites* (GMP 1990).
4. Saunders was eventually released on appeal in 1994.
5. In 1992 a number of gay men were arrested for committing consensual SM sex acts in the notorious police operation 'Spanner'. They were subsequently imprisoned, though the case is now going to the European Court of Human Rights.
6. The early 1990s saw a flurry of 'virgin birth' stories, some of which were to focus on lesbians' right to artificial insemination.
7. *Quim,* Issue 3, Winter 1991.
8. Beth Jordache, a regular character in the Merseyside soap *Brookside,* came out in 1994. The character rapidly reached lesbian icon status. In 1995, Beth was 'killed off' in somewhat dubious circumstances.
9. Tessa Boffin was a photographer and co-editor of *Stolen Glances* (Pandora 1991). She contributed to early *Quim* magazines and was a high-profile member of the SM club scene in London. She died in 1993.

10. Laurence Jaugey-Paget is a photographer and was a regular contributor to *Quim* magazine. She also provided the photographs for *Making Out: The Book of Lesbian Sex and Sexuality* (Pandora 1995).

11. *Butterfly Kiss* by Phyllis Nagy was premiered at the Royal Court in 1994.

12. Sheila Jeffreys, *The Lesbian Heresy* (The Women's Press 1994).

13. 'Lover Girls', in *Time Out* Specail Issue 21–28 June 1995.

14. Christa D'Souza 'Sisters Under the Skin', in *The Sunday Times,* 12 March 1995.

15. Rose Troche, *Go Fish* 1994.

16. Fi Cunningham Reid 1995.

Further Reading

Boffin, T. and Fraser, J. (eds), *Stolen Glances: Lesbians Take Photographs* (Pandora 1991).

Bright, S., *Susie Bright's Sexual Reality: A Virtual Sex World Reader* (Cleis Press 1992).

Bright, S., *Susie Sexpert's Lesbian Sex World* (Cleis Press 1992).

Butler, J., *Gender Trouble* (Routledge 1990).

Califia, P., *Macho Sluts* (Alyson 1988).

Califia, P., *Sapphistry: The Book of Lesbian Sexualit*, 1st edn (Naiad 1980).

Cant, B. and Hemmings, S. (eds), *Radical Records: Thirty Years of Lesbian and Gay History* (Routledge 1988).

Cartledge, S. and Ryan, J. (eds), *Sex and Love* (The Women's Press 1983).

Caster, W., *The Lesbian Sex Book* (Alyson 1993).

Chester, G. and Dickey, J., *Feminism and Censorship* (Prism 1988).

Creith, E., *Undressing Lesbian Sex* (Cassell 1995).

Daly, M., *Gyn/Ecology: The Metaethics of Radical Feminism* (The Women's Press 1979).

Faderman, L., *Odd Girls and Twilight Lovers. A History of Lesbian Life in Twentieth Century America* (Penguin 1992).

Faderman, L., *Surpassing the Love of Men: Romantic Friendship and Love Between Women from the Renaissance to the Present Day* (The Women's Press 1980).

Faludi, S., *Backlash* (Vintage 1992).

Feminist Review, 'Perverse Politics: Lesbian Issues' (Issue 34 1990).

Foucault, M., *The History of Sexuality*, Volume One (Penguin 1984).

Fuss, D. (ed), *Inside/Out Lesbian Theories, Gay Theories* (Routledge 1991).

Hall Carpenter Archives and Lesbian Oral History Group (eds), *Inventing Ourselves: Lesbian Life Stories* (Routledge 1989).

Hall, Radclyffe, *The Well of Loneliness* (Virago 1980).

Hamer, D., and Budge, B. (eds), *The Good, The Bad and The Gorgeous* Pandora 1994).

Harwood, V., Oswell, D., Parkinson, K. and Ward. A. (eds), *Pleasure Principles* (Laurence and Wishart 1993).

Healey, E. and Mason, A. (eds), *Stonewall 25: The Making of the Lesbian and Gay Community in Britain* (Virago 1994).

Higgins, P., *A Queer Reader* (Fourth Estate 1993).

Gibbs, L. (ed), *Daring to Dissent: Lesbian Culture from Margin to Mainstream* (Cassell 1994).

Jeffreys, S., *Anticlimax: A Feminist Perspective on the Sexual Revolution* (The Women's Press 1991).

Jeffreys, S. *The Lesbian Heresy: A Feminist Perspective on the Lesbian Sexual Revolution* (The Women's Press 1994).

Jeffreys, S., *The Spinster and Her Enemies: Feminism and Sexuality 1880–1930* (Pandora Press 1985).

Kennedy, E. and Davis, M. (eds), *Boots of Leather, Slippers of Gold* (Penguin 1994).

Kitzinger, C., *The Social Construction of Lesbianism* (Sage 1987).

Lesbian History Group (eds), *Not a Passing Phase: Reclaiming Lesbians in History 1840-1985* (The Women's Press 1989).

Loulan, J., *Lesbian Sex* (Spinsters 1984).

Loulan, J., *The Lesbian Erotic Dance* (Spinsters 1990).

Mason-John, V., *Talking Black* (Cassell 1995).

Mason-John, V. and Khambatta, A., *Lesbians Talk: Making Black Waves* (Scarlet Press 1993).

Mohin, L., *Love Your Enemy? The Debate Between Heterosexual Feminism and `Political Lesbianism* (Onlywomen Press 1981).

Munt, S. (ed), *New Lesbian Criticism: Literary and Cultural Readings* (Harvester 1992).

Nestle J., *A Restricted Country* (Sheba Feminist Press 1988).

Nestle, J., *The Persistent Desire: A Femme/Butch Reader* (Alyson 1992).

Nestle, J. and Preston, J. (eds), *Sister and Brother* (Cassell 1995).

Plummer, K. (ed.), *The Making of the Modern Homosexual* (Huchinson 1987).

Probyn, E. and Grosz E. (eds), *Sexy Bodies, the Strange Carnalities of Feminism* (Routledge 1995).

Segal, L. and McIntosh, M. (eds), *Sex Exposed: Sexuality and the Pornography Debate* (Virago 1992).

Samois (ed), *Coming to Power* (Alyson 1981).

Schramm-Evans, Z. and Jaugey-Paget, L., *Making Out: The Book of Lesbian Sex and Sexuality* (Pandora 1995).

Sheba Collective (eds), *Serious Pleasure* (Sheba Feminist Publishers 1989).

Sheba Collective (eds), *More Serious Pleasure* (Sheba Feminist Publishers 1990).

Smyth, C., *Lesbians Talk Queer Notions* (Scarlet Press 1992).

Snitow, A., Stansell, C. and Thompson, S. (eds), *Desire: The Politics of Sexuality* (Virago 1983).

Stein, A. (ed), *Sisters, Sexperts, Queers* (Plume Press 1994).

Vance, C. S. (ed.), *Pleasure and Danger: Exploring Female Sexuality* (Pandora Press 1989).

Weeks, J., *Sexuality and its Discontents* (Routledge 1985).

Wilson, E. (with Angela Weir), *Hidden Agendas: Theory, Politics, and Experience in the Women's Movement* (Tavistock 1983).